Praise

'This book is so important … save lives. Despite working harder than ever, people have never been more depressed, anxious and unhappy. Without a doubt, our modern way of life is not working. In fact, it's killing us. But what is to be done? With intelligence and compassion, Headlee presents realistic solutions for how we can reclaim our health and our humanity from a technological revolution that seems hell-bent on destroying both. I'm so grateful to have read this book. It delivers on its promise of a better life' — **Elizabeth Gilbert, author of *Big Magic* and *Eat, Pray, Love***

'*Do Nothing* is a welcome antidote to our toxic hustle culture of burnout. Through deep research and evocative storytelling, Celeste Headlee shows us how to break free from constant pressure and live the life we truly want' — **Arianna Huffington, founder and CEO of Thrive Global**

'Celeste Headlee makes a powerful case that productivity is not an inherent virtue - if you're not careful, it can become a vice. If you've ever felt compelled to work harder, this book is a clarion call to work smarter instead. Sometimes you accomplish more by doing less' — **Adam Grant, *New York Times* bestselling author of *Originals* and *Give and Take*, and host of the chart-topping TED podcast WorkLife**

'At a time when so many people are feeling overworked, overwhelmed and addicted to busyness, work and ever-present technology, Celeste Headlee offers a pathway out. Drawing on extensive research and her own experience, *Do Nothing* is a powerful reminder that taking the time to stop, connect with others and forge real bonds is vital for building community, fostering empathy and ultimately leads to joy' — **Brigid Schulte, author of the *New York* Times bestseller *Overwhelmed*, and director of The Better Life Lab at New America**

'I needed this book. And chances are you need it, too. Celeste Headlee does something amazing in *Do Nothing*. She battles this hectic, stressful time and highlights the things that makes our lives better. Connection. Experience. Self-care. And, above all, she reminds us to get busy living' — **Jared Yates Sexton, author of *The Man They Wanted Me to Be***

'In this thought-provoking, well-researched book, Celeste invites readers to push back against the I'm-too-busy narrative and discover what it means to be truly successful' — **Laura Vanderkam, author of *Off the* Clock and *I Know How She Does It***

This book is honest, heartbreaking and hopeful. It's that kind of gem that you read and know you need to hear, know you need to embrace, even if it's challenging. Incredibly well-researched and yet never preachy or dull, this book will help us all reclaim a bit of our humanness if we allow it' — **Nataly Kogan, author of *Happier Now***

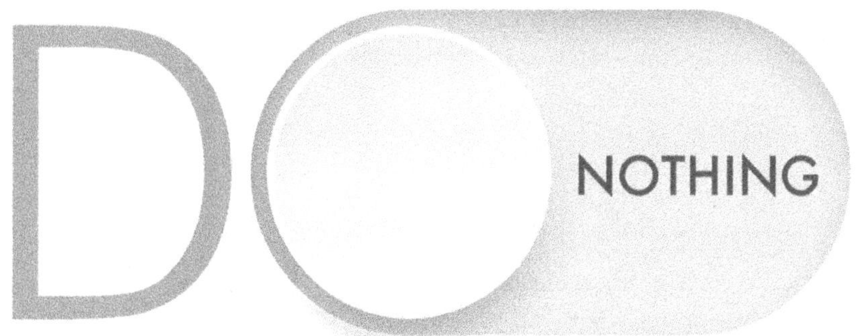

CELESTE HEADLEE

PIATKUS

First published in the US in 2020 by Harmony Books,
an imprint of Penguin Random House LLC
First published in Great Britain in 2020 by Piatkus

1 3 5 7 9 10 8 6 4 2

Some names and identifying details have been changed
to protect the privacy of individuals.

A CIP catalogue record for this book
is available from the British Library.

ISBN 978-0-349-42224-4

Printed and bound in Great Britain by
Clays Ltd, Elcograf SpA

Papers used by Piatkus are from well-managed forests and
other responsible sources.

Piatkus
An imprint of
Little, Brown Book Group
Carmelite House
50 Victoria Embankment
London EC4Y 0DZ

An Hachette UK Company
www.hachette.co.uk

www.improvementzone.co.uk

For Theresa,
who has always been the biggest fan
and the best of friends

CONTENTS

CONTENTS

INTRODUCTION

> It will be said that, while a little leisure is pleasant, men would not know how to fill their days if they had only four hours of work out of the twenty-four. In so far as this is true in the modern world, it is a condemnation of our civilization; it would not have been true at any earlier period. There was formerly a capacity for light-heartedness and play which has been to some extent inhibited by the cult of efficiency. The modern man thinks that everything ought to be done for the sake of something else, and never for its own sake.
>
> —BERTRAND RUSSELL,
> *"In Praise of Idleness," 1932*

WE ANSWER WORK EMAILS on Sunday night. We read endless articles about how to hack our brains to achieve more productivity. We crop our photos and use filters before we post them on social media to earn approval. We read only the first couple paragraphs of the articles we find interesting because we don't have time to read them in their entirety. We are overworked and overstressed, constantly dissatisfied, and reaching for a bar that keeps rising higher and higher. We are members of the cult of efficiency, and we're killing ourselves with productivity.

The passage at the beginning of this Introduction was written in 1932, not long after the stock market crash of 1929, which caused the Great Depression. Russell's description of the "cult of efficiency" predates World War II, the rise of rock and roll, the civil rights movement, and the dawn of the twenty-first century. More important, in my mind: It was written before the creation of the internet and smartphones and social media.

In other words, technology didn't create this cult; it simply added to an existing culture. For generations, we have made ourselves miserable while we've worked feverishly. We have driven ourselves for so long that we've forgotten where we are going, and have lost our capacity for "light-heartedness and play."

Here's the bottom line: We are lonely, sick, and suicidal. Every year a new survey emerges showing more people are isolated and depressed than the year before. It's time to stop watching the trend move in the wrong direction while we throw up our hands in despair. It's time to figure out what's going wrong.

All my life, I've been *driven*. That word has been used to describe me since elementary school.

Driven isn't always a compliment, especially when it's used to describe a woman. It's not quite the same as *ambitious,* and it has a slightly different meaning than *aggressive*. Honestly, I think *driven* fits me fairly well. I've always viewed all forward progress as inherently virtuous and good.

Even as a child, I made long to-do lists in my daily planner (I had a daily planner by the ripe old age of twelve) and made sure I finished more tasks than I added every day. When I was dieting, I motivated myself by saying I would weigh less tomorrow than today, even if it was only by a fraction of an ounce. If I spent an afternoon watching monster movies on TV, I felt guilty. I was terrified that someone would see me sitting idly on the couch and call me lazy.

My drive has helped me succeed in life. It sustained me through single parenthood, layoffs, and physical injury. I've pushed myself to accomplish incredible amounts of work both at home and in my career. But at some point, drive became inextricably intertwined with dread: dread that all my work and effort would never be enough.

Eventually, I got lucky. I achieved much of what I wanted by the time I hit my forties, and I had time to stop, take a breath, and reexamine my way of life. While I'd always been driven, I'd also been exhausted, stressed, and overwhelmed. I assumed depletion was a natural side effect of being a single parent with multiple jobs and not enough money to cover all my expenses. My underlying assumption was that when I achieved financial stability, my stress would end.

That assumption, like so many assumptions, was wrong. My long-dreamed-of moment finally arrived a few years ago: I reached a level of stability that should have made me more comfortable, and I paid off my student loans (at last!). In fact, I paid off every debt I owed. I even had a respectable amount in savings and a real retirement account. I looked forward to nights of relaxation and relief. I expected to feel a lift, an easing of the stress I'd suffered for two decades, but that relief never came.

My daily planner (still an old-school one with paper pages) was as packed with tasks as it was before I'd paid off my debts, if not more so. My workload was as heavy with one job as it was when I had four. In the evenings, I was as worn out and exhausted as ever.

I realized it was not my circumstances that caused my stress but my habits. While my list of duties got shorter at the office, I found new duties to fill the empty space and called more meetings. At home, I decided I finally had time to make my own bread and learn Spanish. Instead of cooking the tried-and-true favorites in my recipe book, I searched the internet for new and exotic dishes that required an hour of driving in order to gather the ingredients. I agreed to serve on two advisory boards and chose to start writing a blog. And every week, I collapsed onto my couch on Friday night and thought about how I used to meet my friends for drinks, but now I didn't have time.

I had some tough questions for myself. Why? Why do I do this? Why do any of us do this?

For the past several years, I've searched for the answer to those questions. Reading that eighty-seven-year-old essay from Bertrand Russell brought a flash of insight. I considered the fact that I did things rarely for their own sake, but in service to my drive to constantly improve and be productive. Far too many of us have been lured into the cult of efficiency. We are driven, but we long ago lost sight of what we were driving toward. We judge our days based on how efficient they are, not how fulfilling.

We search for the best method of doing everything, from holding meetings to exercising to barbecuing, and we are lured by the "ultimate tools" to improve our lives. We are like mechanics who build a car by assembling the top-of-the-line parts, focused only on finding the best of everything and not on whether those parts work well together. The end result is a car that struggles to start and keeps stalling out.

What is the cult of efficiency? It's a group whose members believe fervently in the virtue of constant activity, in finding the most efficient way to accomplish just about anything and everything. They are busy all the time and they take it on faith that all their effort is saving time and making their lives better.

But they're wrong. The efficiency is an illusion. They believe they're being efficient when they're actually wasting time.

Imagine that you need to learn how to swim. You read books on swimming, you buy a DVD series on the subject, you participate in a webinar about it. Maybe you install several apps on your phone that track your swim time and help you find the nearest pool. You do everything you can to learn how to swim except get into the water.

More and more, this is our approach to problem-solving.

We are investing our time and energy and hard-earned money in things we think will make us more efficient, but those things end up wasting our time, exhausting us, and stressing us out without bringing us closer to our goals. We take extraordinary measures to become more productive, only to become less so. Is there a good explanation?

The human drive to constantly improve and grow is innate and, in most ways, commendable. The modern human has been around for only about 300,000 years (compare that to the 66 million years or so that dinosaurs existed), and yet we've come a long way from the mud huts of the first *Homo sapiens.*

We have endured incredible hardship and unspeakable tragedy, but we developed a coping mechanism to prevent us from slipping into despair. It's called the hedonic treadmill. It's a tendency in our species to adjust our mood so that no matter what terrible things happen, we quickly return to the same level of happiness we enjoyed before the traumatic event.

There's a catch, though: It also works in reverse. In other words, if an incredibly happy change occurs in our lives, we don't move forward as happier people. Instead, the hedonic treadmill brings us right back to the state of mind we were in before the raise in pay, new house, or lost weight. It means that, for many of us, we are never satisfied.

Imagine you finally earn a million dollars. Euphoria ensues, right? Wrong. Your mind will adjust and send you right back to your happiness set point. As Dr. Alex Lickerman, author of *The Undefeated Mind: On the Science of Constructing an Indestructible Self,* explains, "Our level of happiness may change transiently in response to life events, but then almost always returns to its baseline level as we habituate to those events and their consequences over time."

That makes us all vulnerable to those who promise more happiness and a better life through the use of their product, system, or software. We crave more joy and satisfaction. No matter what we achieve, no matter how many extra hours we work, we remain unfulfilled. As the nineteenth-century economist Henry George wrote, a human is "the only animal whose desires increase as they are fed; the only animal that is never satisfied."

For the past five hundred years or so, we've searched for external solutions to our internal problem. We have been deluded by the forces of economics and religion to believe that the purpose of life is hard work. So every time we feel empty, dissatisfied, or unfulfilled, we work harder and put in more hours. This trend can be traced to Martin Luther's Ninety-Five Theses, Christopher Columbus, and the Age of Discovery. With Luther, laziness became a sin, and with Columbus and the Age of Discovery, the developed world's eyes turned to new and unfamiliar places, to novelty as an end goal.

These obsessions became widespread during the industrial age and they have only strengthened in the more than two centuries since. Our time periods are not named for human development anymore, like the Renaissance and the Enlightenment. We are currently in the jet age, the information age, the nuclear age, and the Digital Revolution. We measure our years in work products, not personal development.

Ultimately, the solution is not digital. It is as analog as the human body. Technology can do many things for us—extend our lives, keep us safe, expand our entertainment options—but it cannot make us happy. The key to well-being is shared humanity, even though we are pushing further and further toward separation.

We don't seem to trust our human instincts. When we're faced with a difficult problem, we search for the right tech, the right tool, and the right system that will solve the issue: bulletproof coffee, punishing exercise, paleo diets, goal-tracking journals, productivity apps. We think our carefully designed strategies and gadgets will make us better. My goal is to dispel that illusion and help you to see that we are not better, but in many cases, worse.

I know it feels as though we don't have a choice in the matter, that we would work less if we could, but that's not entirely true. Here in the States, we're particularly bad about taking time off. We chose not to take 705 million vacation days in

2017, and more than 200 million of those were lost forever because they couldn't be carried over to the next year. That means Americans donated $62 billion to their employers in one year. The number of vacation days we use has declined over the past three decades, even though those who use all of their time off report being 20 percent happier in their relationships and 56 percent happier in general.

Since the nineteenth century at least, we've learned this behavior from the previous generation and then added to it before passing on the lessons to the next generation. We are teaching this mind-set to our kids and inculcating them into the cult. When asked, most parents say they just want their kids to be happy. And yet research reveals that what most parents actually want is high GPAs, because they think success in school will make their kids happy.

Let's take a breath. Consider for just a moment what we know about the essential nature of humankind. Superficially, we are upright, talking great apes. According to where we live, we look different, speak differently, and value very different things, but is there such a thing as a true human nature that spans all continents and cultures? Are there qualities that we share from birth, regardless of our nationality, faith, or income? Just how much of our behavior is controlled by biology and how much by individual circumstance and environment is a long-standing topic of fierce debate among scientists.

Still, there are a few things that all humans can learn to do well without training: play, think, connect socially, react emotionally, count, and think about ourselves. Perhaps we take them for granted, since we don't often invest much energy in those activities. Perhaps, because they are inherent to most of us, we assume our ability to fit into a community is a given. So over the past decade, we've found "better" things to do with our time.

Few of our daily activities are focused on helping us become more naturally playful or thoughtful or, god forbid, social. Our social networks are no substitute for the intimate connections we have made for 200,000 years, and our work schedules don't allow for play.

Essentially, we are working our way out of happiness and well-being. We've lost the balance between striving to improve and feeling gratitude for what we have. We've lost touch with the things that really enrich our lives and make us feel content. We've spent billions of dollars in the past decade or so finding replacements for what we as human beings already do well.

At this point, this toxic trend has gone too far. What began a couple hundred years ago has taken ahold of our lives both at work and at home. We are digging deeper and deeper into a hole that will eventually bury us if we don't stop. The stakes could not possibly be higher. We are talking about the loss of our own humanity.

According to numerous surveys, social isolation has doubled among many adults since the 1990s, and social isolation is deadly. The United Kingdom created a new government position in 2017: Minister of Loneliness. Suicide rates among teens in the United States were on the decline for years but started rising dramatically in 2010 and are still on the rise. How is this possible in a world that is more connected than ever? In an age in which even the most remote areas of the world can generally get a package from Amazon in a few days' time?

Part of the problem is that we're cutting out expressions of our basic humanity because they're "inefficient": boredom, long phone conversations, hobbies, neighborhood barbecues, membership in social clubs. We smile indulgently at the naivetés of the past, when people had time for things like pickup basketball and showing slides of Hawaiian vacations to their friends. How quaint, we think, that our grandparents had time for things like sewing circles and lawn bowling.

But wouldn't our ancestors have had less time than we do? After all, we have microwaves and dishwashers and gas lawnmowers and the internet! We can order just about anything and get it delivered to our door. We have robot vacuums and AI assistants that tell us the weather and set our alarms. If you add up all the time saved through technological advancement over the past one hundred years, shouldn't we have hours of excess time in which to do as we please?

Why are we so efficient and yet so overwhelmed? Why are we so productive with so little to show for it?

I think we have engineered our way further and further from what we do best and what makes us most human. In doing so, we've made our lives harder and infinitely sadder. "I can hunch over my computer screen for half the day churning frenetically through emails without getting much of substance done," writes Dan Pallotta in the *Harvard Business Review,* "all the while telling myself what a loser I am, and leave at 6:00 p.m. feeling like I put in a full day. And given my level of mental fatigue, I did!"

Many of us are exhausting ourselves this way, working very hard at things that accomplish very little of substance but feel necessary. To a large extent, the solution to this problem is to correct our misperceptions. In the way that those with body dysmorphia see something other than the truth in the mirror, the *feeling* of being productive is not the same as actually producing something. The truth is, overwork reduces productivity. The Greeks work more hours than any other Europeans, according to data from the OECD (Organisation for Economic Cooperation and Development). Yet they rank twenty-fourth out of twenty-five nations for productivity.

Perhaps some of the systems we adopt are unnecessary. After all, humans do many things beautifully without assistance or intervention. Without medication or yoga, we can relieve stress and induce feelings of happiness. Research shows you can lift your mood simply by taking a walk; no need to track your steps.

I'd like to inspire a new consideration of leisure and a new appreciation for idleness. Idleness in this sense does not mean inactivity, but instead nonproductive activity. "Leisureliness," says Daniel Dustin of the University of Utah, "refers to a pace of life that is not governed by the clock. It tends to run counter to the notions of economic efficiency, economies of scale, mass production, etc. Yet leisureliness to me suggests slowing down and milking life for all it is worth." That's the kind of leisure I hope we can all make time for. It's what humans were meant to enjoy and what we need in order to function at our highest levels.

To embrace leisure, we don't have to let go of progress. My argument is not that we are moving too fast or changing too quickly. In fact, I'm saying quite the opposite. I believe our constant pushing is now impeding our progress.

We work best when we allow for flexibility in our habits. Instead of gritting your teeth and forcing your body and mind to work punishing hours and "lean in" until you reach your goals, the counterintuitive solution might be to walk away. Pushing harder isn't helping us anymore.

We can and must stop treating ourselves like machines that can be driven and pumped and amped and hacked. Instead of limiting and constraining our essential natures, we can celebrate our humanness at work *and* in idleness. We can better understand our own natures and abilities. We can lean in not to our work but to our inherent gifts.

PART I

The Cult of Efficiency

Chapter 1

MIND THE GAP

> Rhythm is sound in motion. It is related to the pulse, the heartbeat, the way we breathe. It rises and falls. It takes us into ourselves, it takes us out of ourselves.
>
> —EDWARD HIRSCH

LET'S START WITH A conversation about pace. For a musician, pace is the speed and rhythm of a piece of music. For all of us, pace is the speed and rhythm of our lives. *Fast-paced* generally has a good connotation in the modern world, and there's certainly nothing wrong with getting things done quickly.

I'd love to visit the doctor without waiting for an hour past my scheduled appointment, and I nearly lose my mind when I'm stuck in traffic and trying to get home. Involuntary slowdowns are infuriating. What's more, tools that shorten the time it takes to do something unpleasant are welcome. A better dishwasher that eliminates the need to wash dishes by hand? Yes, please. An app that allows me to check in to a hotel while I'm still at the airport? Absolutely.

But what about the pace of things we love to do? What about *voluntary* slowdowns? It could be that in searching for ways to get things done faster, we also shorten the time we spend doing fun things like hiking or completing crossword puzzles. Is it always desirable to go faster, get to places quicker, increase speed, and reduce the time it takes to accomplish something? Or are there inherent benefits to slowing down from time to time?

These are the questions I began to ask myself last year, when I was fighting my second bout of bronchitis in eight months. "Get some rest," my doctor said. "Sit and read a book or watch a movie, but do not go in to work."

I didn't follow her advice. I was the host of a daily radio show and I had to be on the air Monday through Friday. I also had speaking engagements nearly every week that required travel. My typical schedule: Rise at 4:30 a.m., host my radio show until 10:00 a.m., go to the airport, fly to whatever city I'd be speaking in, go to sleep, rise the next morning and give a keynote speech, fly home and go to sleep, rise the next day at 4:30 a.m. in order to host the radio show.

All the while, I was doing podcast interviews to support my book, writing pieces for various publications, and occasionally appearing on the BBC to talk about news in the States. I rarely saw my son, and when I did, I was cranky. All I wanted to do in my spare time was scooch into a corner of the couch and watch sitcoms.

I started to wonder if I was moving too fast, so fast that I didn't have time to make rational decisions about what things I wanted to do and what things I was doing just because they appeared on my calendar. I realized that I was in automatic mode. I was like Lucy in that famous episode at the chocolate factory, except that I kept speeding up to keep pace with the conveyor belt of events in my life.

"Do you sometimes think we try to do too much at once?" I asked one of my mentors.

"I used to do that," he answered. "And then I started making sure there was space in my calendar, enough space to allow air in so that I could breathe."

I mentioned my concerns to another friend and she directed me to Carl Honoré's TED talk on the Slow Movement. Honoré didn't start the movement—his talk and book came years after the idea had sprung up in Italy and started to spread worldwide. But his thoughts on the subject were certainly compelling.

The Slow Movement started out as a protest against fast food. You have probably seen pictures of the Piazza di Spagna in Rome. It's the open area at the bottom of the Spanish Steps, and in the middle of the cobbled square is the famous Fontana della Barcaccia (Fountain of the Old Boat), created by Pietro Bernini in the early 1600s.

The fountain design was based on a legend. In the sixteenth century, it was said that the river Tiber overflowed its banks and when the waters subsided, a solitary boat was left in the center of that square. In honor of that story, Bernini crafted a boat out of travertine that seems to be floating in clear water.

The poet John Keats lived in a house on the Piazza di Spagna until his death, and the house is open to the public now as a museum. A grand 135-step staircase on one side of the square leads up to the Church of the Trinità dei Monti. All in all, it is a beautiful spot in Rome, historically significant, and justifiably treasured by the Italian people.

So in the 1980s, when McDonald's announced its intention to build a restaurant in the Piazza di Spagna, some people protested. Notable among the protesters was a thin, blue-eyed man named Carlo Petrini.

Petrini was a well-established food critic, and when McDonald's opened its doors, he distributed bowls of penne to the crowds of protesters and founded a group called Slow Food.

The organization's manifesto declares, "We are enslaved by speed and have all succumbed to the same insidious virus: Fast Life."

The group encourages people to enjoy the process of preparing food, of tasting every bite, of enjoying conversation with others at the table. There are now Slow Food chapters in more than 150 countries.

Slow Food has spread and sparked other efforts, such as the farm-to-table movement, but the underlying ideas about pace have spread to nongastronomic industries, such as fashion, education, and travel.

The idea is not that everything should be slower, but that not everything needs to be fast. I fly tens of thousands of miles every year for my work, and I have no desire to lengthen any of those business trips by choosing twenty-one hours on a train instead of four hours in a plane.

But if I'm going to New Orleans to visit friends, I might bypass the extra time spent getting to the airport, going through the security line, waiting at the gate, and catching a taxi to my hotel and instead choose to hop on a train. It's slower, but I get to my destination in a better mood (train travel is infinitely less stressful for me than using airlines).

Believe me, this is not a case of someone with limitless amounts of free time admonishing you to go out and smell the roses. Not only do I identify with the compulsion to move as quickly as possible, but I've indulged that compulsion for most of my life. Of course, I'm acutely aware that I'm now self-employed and therefore not beholden to someone else's schedule, but I began to explore the idea of slowing down select portions of my life while I was still employed full-time.

After experimenting with the idea, I realized that throttling back was possible in a number of areas. I found that I was able to cook from scratch if I limited the number of interviews I did each week. By staying away from social media between the hours of eight in the morning and five in the evening, I could fit in an extra walk with my dog. But those small changes were not enough for me.

The most significant reason that I resigned from my full-time position and started my own company was a desire to gain control of my time. I was so busy that I felt my work was controlling my life and dictating all of my decisions, and I knew that it wasn't making me happier.

I thought a relaxed schedule would happen automatically when I became my own boss, but it didn't. Once I stopped spending forty to fifty hours at the radio station every week, I simply added forty hours' worth (or more) of other events and tasks to my calendar to fill the gap. My thought process went something like this: I'm not working full-time anymore, so I can do that extra speaking engagement or write a couple more articles. The result was that I had more on my schedule as a freelancer than I did when I was working for someone else! In other words, my boss wasn't really the problem.

It's not that I've mastered this issue and am therefore writing a book to tell you how to do what I did. I struggle with it every day, and my book research was originally intended to help me solve my own problem.

When I began to read about the Slow Movement, I understood immediately how a slower pace might reduce my stress and support a sense of mindfulness. I did much of that research in July 2018. Clearly, the information didn't stick, because just a few months later, in October, I did six different thirty-to-sixty-minute podcast interviews and six speaking engagements in Atlanta, Chicago, Los Angeles, Toronto, Palm Springs, and Washington, DC.

Let me stop here for just a moment and acknowledge a very privileged elephant in the room: I'm a very lucky person. After forty-six years of struggle, living paycheck to paycheck as a single mom, lightning struck for me in 2016. My TEDx Talk went viral and I started getting offers to deliver speeches for the kind of pay that I didn't dare dream of in years prior.

Before 2016, I was working punishing hours and living in a state of constant stress, worrying about bills and whether I could handle a hypothetical financial emergency. After 2016, I was still working ridiculous hours and feeling exhausted and overwhelmed, but I was well paid. Not having to worry about paying rent, not living in dread that I might break my arm or my car might stop working, made a significant improvement to my overall well-being.

There is no denying that having enough money makes things much easier. But throughout all those years of struggle, I thought life with more money would mean happiness and an end to stress. That didn't happen.

Most of my business travel is well planned by an assistant, with drivers to and from the airport and stays in hotels I couldn't afford for most of my life. The 2015 Celeste would have looked at me today and said, "What the hell do you have to complain about? You're lucky you're not climbing onto a bus because you can't afford a taxi. Suck it up." But 2018 Celeste had to edit four scripts and do two podcast interviews before dinnertime, and she didn't feel very privileged. Actually, she was miserable.

It became clear that no change would occur in my life simply because I wanted it. I had to take concrete steps and set up new limits. As the ancient Greeks would say: Physician, heal thyself.

In January 2019, I embarked on a train trip around the entire contiguous forty-eight states. I rode one train from DC to New Orleans, another to Los Angeles, and a third up to Seattle. Then I took a train to Chicago, one more to Boston, and then boarded the final train that took me home to DC. The entire trip took nearly two weeks.

Keep in mind that cross-country trains often travel through remote areas, where cell signals are faint or nonexistent. The first time I looked at my cell phone and saw the big circle with the line through it instead of signal bars, I admit that I felt panicked. I started obsessively checking my phone to see if I had a connection yet. I probably checked it forty times in an hour, and that was only the second day of a two-week trip.

As more days passed, I relaxed. I survived for hours without a cell signal and nothing exploded. No emergencies cropped up; everything was okay. Two weeks without any reliable connection to the internet allowed me the space to assess whether I needed to be constantly connected, and it turns out the answer is no.

It's a very simple thing, to step on a train and stop worrying about the time it takes to travel, but in this age of escalation and ever-increasing speeds, it felt like a revolutionary act. I had several offers to deliver speeches during those two weeks and could have earned a significant amount of money, but instead I sat in a railcar chatting with folks and reading mystery novels. In the end, I think I chose the most valuable use of my time.

I felt transformed as I sat in the final train, headed south to my home in DC. I don't think I checked my watch once, because I wasn't worried about what time we were going to arrive. I wrote and read and chatted a little with the guy across the aisle. The sense that something could go wrong at any time, or that something urgent would arise that might require my immediate attention, was gone. I was no longer in fight-or-flight mode. Breaking away from the relentless pace of connected life felt uncomfortable at first, but as I ended my trip, I dreaded joining that joyless parade again.

"Slow travel now rivals the fly-to-Barcelona-for-lunch culture," Carl Honoré says. "Advocates savour the journey, travelling by train or boat or bicycle, or even on foot, rather than crammed into an airplane. They take time to plug into the local culture instead of racing through a list of tourist traps."

What I learned is that if you don't consciously choose a slower path, you will likely default to the pedal-to-the-metal speeds of modern life. It's not a matter of saying that you plan to slow down, because everyone and everything around you might be zooming by. Most of us instinctively keep pace with our environment.

It's also not necessary to go to the opposite extreme. I don't have to sit on a train for days at a time to experience a slower pace. This morning, I arrived at the Atlanta airport with about ninety minutes to kill before my flight. So I bypassed the passenger train and walked to my terminal. *Why,* I thought, *do I want to rush in order to sit at my gate for an extra twenty minutes anyway?*

Along the way, I saw dozens of large-scale sculptures by artists in Zimbabwe and enjoyed one of my favorite art installations of all time, *Flight Paths* by Steve Waldeck. When you pass from terminal A to B, you walk through a simulation of a tropical rainforest, with the sounds of distant birds and a warm summer rain shower. This $4.1 million kinetic light sculpture is guaranteed to make you feel more relaxed.

There was a young mother and her daughter walking fairly slowly ahead of me. My first reaction was irritation, and I nearly stepped to the side so I could walk briskly by. Then I remembered that I had plenty of time, and so I slowed my pace to match the little girl's. It brought up memories of walking with my son when he was a toddler, how I had often felt pressured to hurry him or pick him up so we wouldn't delay others behind us.

I relaxed my steps just a little and was able to watch the girl's amazement as she traveled through the rainforest installation. "You can hear birds, Mom," she cried. "Are they real birds?" I hope that by choosing not to hasten by the pair, I had prevented that mother from feeling pressure to rush her little girl.

This was a small change that cost me only a few minutes, and yet I arrived at my gate with a smile on my face. When was the last time I felt happy and relaxed at the airport? It may have been one small decision that brought me only a half hour of enjoyment, but if I made more decisions like it, I could begin to string together moments of tranquility until, eventually, the balance of my life would tilt away from anxiety and toward refreshment.

Of course, making those decisions isn't always as easy as we'd like it to be.

I come from an accomplished line of overachievers, and I'm not nearly the most impressive leaf on my family tree. Obviously, something inside me compels me to work harder, even when I don't need to. Could it be because of my upbringing?

I considered the habits of my siblings, my mother, and my grandparents. I read what I could about my great-grandmother, Carrie Still Shepperson, who was born to an enslaved woman and fathered by a plantation owner. She got her teaching degree at Atlanta University in 1886. She taught for years at Union School, the first school for black kids in Little Rock, Arkansas. After her first husband's death, she was a single mother for nearly a decade before she remarried. Single motherhood is difficult now; I cannot imagine how hard it must have been for a black woman in the South in 1895.

Carrie also opened the first library for African Americans in Arkansas, and she raised the money to do it by staging productions of Shakespeare and other classics. She spent many weekends traveling into the rural communities of Arkansas to teach black people there how to read and write, and when she passed away in 1927, my grandfather found she'd written a book, which remains unpublished.

Suffice it to say, no one would dare call Carrie Still Shepperson a slacker. And yet when I read about her daily life, it looked remarkably relaxed to my twenty-first-century eyes. She listened to opera on the family's Victrola, she read poetry with friends at Lotus Club meetings, she had plenty of time to mold the young mind of her precocious son, and she ate dinner with her family every night, often cooked by her mother, who had spent most of her life as a slave in Georgia.

It's ludicrous and cruel to talk about work ethic in the same breath as slavery, so I'm looking only as far back as my first free ancestor. She was, by any measure, a fierce and tireless woman. She drilled the principles of hard work into my grandfather, who taught them to my mother, who irritated my younger self by telling me to "at least do something while you're watching TV. Don't just sit there."

My great-grandparents on my father's side were farmers in Texas. I'm sure they toiled in tough conditions and lived by a belief in labor and good works. And yet they too filled their days with chats around the dinner table and card games and fish frys and handicrafts. My grandfather used to make homemade ice cream in his driveway, churning while I sat on the lid to keep it steady.

Research into my own family's past taught me two things: First, the belief in the inherent value of constant productivity dates back to at least the late nineteenth century. Second, we used to temper long hours with equal amounts of leisure and social gatherings. So, this way of being started a long time ago and has become more ingrained and extreme with ensuing generations.

If I wanted to find the source of my addiction to efficiency, I'd have to hit the history books. I began reading about labor practices in the 1950s, the 1920s, the turn of the twentieth century, going further and further back to find the original culprit. Eventually, I began to read about daily life in the 1600s and stretched back to ancient Greece. I realized that work habits were almost wholly different up to about 250 years ago. I had an epiphany: Everything we think we know about work and efficiency and leisure is relatively recent and very possibly wrong.

Chapter 2

IT STARTS WITH A STEAM ENGINE

> The tempo of life was slow, even leisurely; the pace of work relaxed. Our ancestors may not have been rich, but they had an abundance of leisure.
>
> —JULIET SCHOR, SOCIOLOGIST

WORKING FOR PAY IS a very old concept, but perhaps not as old as you might guess. As recently as 9,000 years ago, humans lived communally on land that was shared, and they harvested crops that fed an entire community. The anthropologist Ian Hodder of Stanford says these people probably didn't think of their chores as work, and instead saw them "as just part of their daily activities, along with cooking, rituals and feasts that were such an important part of their lives."

Who knows when the first person decided to bribe someone else to do what they didn't want to do, but we have a record of one of those early transactions. The first paycheck dates back

5,000 years to a city in what is now Iraq. In exchange for their labor, someone was paid in beer (an ancient Homer Simpson from Mesopotamia, perhaps). Since then, putting in hours in exchange for beer or food or another type of pay has been fairly common all over the world.

It's possible, though, that we've operated for a long time using an incorrect idea about what "work" meant for our ancestors. Medieval peasants worked, on average, far fewer hours than we do today, and they enjoyed significantly more vacation time. It may feel as though we've always had to work at least forty hours a week in order to make a living, but that's actually a relatively recent phenomenon.

I'm not about to make the case that people were better off in the Middle Ages. That's obviously not true. Most people have a much higher quality of life now, and we are in little danger of dying from the plague. We are significantly more likely to survive childhood, our homes are more comfortable, and we have better access to education in most places. Certainly, we are mostly better off than the average European peasant in the 1600s. But we do, in general, work longer hours. That's an indisputable fact.

For our purposes, I'm only talking about working hours and nonworking hours. I'm not including the amount of time it takes to do laundry and cook meals and travel, even though that is work. I'm referring only to the amount of time people spend earning what is needed in order to survive. Work can be enjoyable and fulfilling, or it can be repetitive and dull, but it is always something we are compelled to do, out of necessity. As it turns out, in a side-by-side comparison between today and the Middle

Ages, it took far fewer hours of work in order to support a peasant in 1600 than it does to support the average employee today.

In fact, for most of the 300,000 years (give or take) that *Homo sapiens* has been walking upright around the world, we did not work forty hours a week, and we certainly didn't work more than three hundred days a year. Our working habits changed dramatically a little more than two centuries ago. Modern work hours are an aberration, and we have enough historical record to be able to prove that.

Going back as far as 4,000 years ago, to the days of ancient Greece, we find that Athenians had up to sixty holidays a year. By the middle of the fourth century BC, there were nearly six months of official festival days, on which no work was done. Work for the ancient Greeks was carried out in spurts: intense activity during planting or harvest, followed by extended periods of rest for celebrations and feasts.

For much of Europe, Asia, and North Africa, that basic model remained mostly unchanged for tens of thousands of years. Before the industrial age began in Britain in 1760, most people lived by the same habits their ancestors had going back to the time of Plato and Aristotle. Their day began with the sunrise and ended as the fiery star disappeared below the horizon. Human life paralleled that of the birds.

Up to the nineteenth century, only the wealthy could afford to burn candles on a regular basis, so sundown meant darkness. Athens had about fourteen daylight hours in summer and nearly ten in the winter.

Certainly, fourteen hours is a long day of work. But Homer's household staff didn't work a fourteen-hour day. The English historian and economist James E. Thorold Rogers wrote extensively about the habits of the working class through six hundred years of British history. According to his research, medieval peasants worked no more than eight hours a day, sometimes less, and spent at least a third of the year off work, celebrating saints' days and other special events.

I want to add another disclaimer here: I have no interest in traveling back in time to live as a serf in medieval England. I like my electric car and my microwave and my computer very much, thank you. But it's not just technology that's changed over the course of time; it's also lifestyle and quality of life. Up until two hundred years ago, we had a lot more time off. In the preindustrial world, work was not the axis around which all life turned.

As Thorold Rogers wrote in his book *Six Centuries of Work and Wages,* "The age had its drawbacks, as every age has, but it had its advantages . . . the peasant of the thirteenth century, though he did not possess . . . much that his descendant had in the eighteenth, had some solid elements of present advantage and not a few hopes of future advancement."

The hope of future advancement resided in the ability to either work your own land or gain income as a craftsman or artisan. Prior to the dawn of the industrial age, most people were self-employed or worked as contractors and so were able to make their own schedules.

In the book *Life on the English Manor,* H. S. Bennett notes that under the feudal system, most serfs owed "day-a-week" dues to their lord. That equals one day's labor, with work beginning in the morning and lasting until lunch. That's about six and a half hours during the summer. Artisans worked about nine hours a day, Bennett found, but worked for themselves, had complete flexibility in their work hours, and kept nearly all of their profits. Farmers tending their own crops worked a little more than eight hours a day.

Until the nineteenth century, working fifty-two weeks a year was nearly unheard of anywhere in the world. Laborers had so much time off that James Pilkington, bishop of Durham, complained about it in the early sixteenth century: "The laboring man will take his rest long in the morning," the bishop wrote. "A good piece of the day is spent afore he come at his work; then he must have his breakfast, though he have not earned it at his accustomed hour, or else there is drudging and murmuring. . . . At noon he must have his sleeping time, then his bever in the afternoon, which spendeth a great part of the day; and when his hour cometh at night, at the first stroke of the clock he casteth down his tools, leaveth his work, in what need or case soever the work standeth."

The bishop wasn't the only annoyed aristocrat. There are a variety of surviving examples of wealthy people complaining that workers were lazy and took too much time off. That, at least, hasn't changed at all.

This all predates the age of factories and machinery, of course. The shifts in culture, economics, politics, and labor in the nineteenth century were massive. It's impossible to overstate how significantly the Industrial Revolution changed every aspect of human life, including the kind of food people ate and how long they slept at night.

Before the 1800s, working life was basically the same stretching back for centuries. Most people lived in rural areas, many owned or leased at least a small plot of land, and they had lots of time to handle their own household or work their own land. They actually had time to sit around a fire and listen to all 3,182 lines of an epic poem like *Beowulf.* Back then, that was considered a fun night with the family.

Although we have very good records of labor practices in England, we also know that the other European nations were fairly similar in their approach to leisure time. In her book *The Overworked American,* the sociologist Juliet Schor notes that the English worked more than their neighbors. In France, laborers were guaranteed 180 days of rest, and in Spain, workers were entitled to about five months' respite a year.

The exceptions, in all areas, were slaves and some indentured servants. We're not sure when Africans were first forced into slavery, but we know slaves were legally owned by 1640. When I talk about working hours, I'm not talking about slaves, who had no power or input and were not trading labor for wages. Slavery was barbaric for a number of reasons, including its characterization of some human beings as worthy of no more respect or care than a horse or cow.

In this history of labor practices, I'm speaking not of specific populations but generally about the working class, those who are employed by others for wages.

Because we have detailed records of labor practices in Britain and the rest of Europe, that's where I've focused most of my attention. I don't intend to imply that all people everywhere experienced what Europeans did, or that the European system was in any way superior.

However, many of us who live in industrialized nations now are still following the traditions and customs formed in Britain and the rest of Europe. Many employers, artisans, and government officials in those regions kept careful records of what days people worked and what days were set aside for leisure. That's how I know that human life for tens of millions of people changed with the dawn of the industrial era. It's also how I know that at least some of that change was not positive.

Many different influences led society from the Enlightenment to the industrial age. People were living longer by the late 1700s, so labor was plentiful, and the Agricultural Revolution brought a surplus of food to Britain, so many people who had been employed on farms were suddenly looking for work. What's more, innovations in banking, trade, and transportation made it easier to do business year-round and across international borders.

And yet perhaps the most direct stimulus of the industrial era occurred in Scotland at the University of Glasgow, when a mostly self-taught instrument maker named James Watt was asked to repair a Newcomen steam engine. He fixed it, but found the engine still put out very little power.

So he started fiddling with the machinery and experimenting with steam until he developed a model that used 75 percent less fuel than the Newcomen and was considerably more powerful. More than a decade later, in 1776, as John Adams and Thomas Jefferson were signing the Declaration of Independence in Philadelphia, the first Watt engines were being sold commercially and installed in Great Britain.

The Watt steam engine was originally used, mostly, for pumping water out of coal mines, but it didn't take long for people to realize you could attach the engines to just about anything. Looms became steam powered, as did mills and foundries. Cities no longer needed a river and a waterwheel to generate power, nor did they need hundreds of horses. (Remember that *horsepower* used to be a literal term.) Factories were built, steamships appeared on the Thames, and the industrial age began.

When factories began to produce goods, the nature of employment was transformed. Before the nineteenth century, most people lived in rural areas. By 1850, for the first time in world history, more British people lived in cities than in the countryside. It took another seventy years before that milestone was passed in the United States, around the same time that Buster Keaton was a movie star and people were dancing the Charleston.

Prior to the industrial age, most people worked to complete specific tasks: bring in the harvest, put up the barn, stitch a quilt. Over the course of a day, a farmer might accomplish a vast variety of tasks: tending animals, watering crops, trapping pests, repairing fences, and any number of other duties. When those farmers became factory workers, they lost the variety in their working days and ended up performing the same mindless, monotonous task while standing in the same position for ten to fourteen hours a day.

Another change was in the ubiquity of ownership. Historians have noted that in England, at least, most people during the Middle Ages owned some land. Serfs had a minimum of twelve acres and cultivated their own crops. Over the past 250 years, public lands have become privately owned; there are no more cows grazing on the commons anymore. This is what drove the exodus from homes in the countryside to crowded rooms in urban areas.

Most cities were not prepared to accommodate these massive influxes of residents. As people crammed into cities, their houses became "a mass of filth and misery," the historian E. P. Thompson noted. What's more, a worker who rented a wretched room in London was considerably less powerful than a serf who owned even a tiny plot of land in the country. The move to cities drained power and wealth from the working classes.

When people began to labor in factories, there was no end to the work. You weren't making one carriage wheel to replace a broken one—you were churning out dozens of carriage wheels. You could continue making shirts or horseshoes or water buckets or ink bottles until you ran out of resources or you couldn't lift your arms anymore, and you were replaced by someone else who picked up where you left off.

Business profits were suddenly based more on volume of sales and less on profit margins. "Companies now needed workers' time to labour in the factories and clock time to coordinate the masses to keep the wheels of industry turning," the business psychologist Tony Crabbe points out. "So valuable had time become that many unscrupulous business owners would adjust their clocks during the day to get more hours out of their unsuspecting labourers."

Here's another point to consider: Until the late 1800s, most European economies contained a sizable craftsman class: tinkers, farriers, leatherworkers, and others who owned their own tools and were masters of their chosen field. If you wanted to build a cathedral, you hired workmen to put up the walls and artisans to carve railings and sculpt gargoyles and paint altars.

As the historian Nelson Lichtenstein points out, Paul Revere was an accomplished silversmith, and the familiar portrait of him that now hangs in the Boston Museum of Fine Arts was painted seven years before his famous ride. In it, he's dressed in shirtsleeves and has dirt under his fingernails. Craftsmen were respected and mostly independent.

As the industrial era chugged ahead, craftsmen were pulled into the factories. A glassblower couldn't compete with a glass factory. So he sold his tools and took up a position on a factory floor, where the instruments and machinery were owned not by workers but by the employer. When a worker left a job, he no longer took with him the means to find new work. He relied entirely on a new employer to supply the tools and the resources. Again, this was a significant transfer of power.

Because of this shift, the world lost many of its specialized artists and woodworkers and sculptors and metalsmiths. (Here's an interesting exercise: Take a look at some pictures of England's Houses of Parliament, built between 1839 and 1842. Imagine how much it would cost to have all that work done today and you'll understand one aspect of what was abandoned when we lost our craftsman class.) In factories, workers usually didn't develop the same pride in their work as they churned out dozens of items every day.

Also, social mobility stagnated. Before the nineteenth century, it was possible to learn a trade and work your way into the middle class. But factories don't need tradesmen—they need bodies and hands, and there are just a handful of managerial positions available. There was very little opportunity for promotion or advancement during the nineteenth century, and it became nearly impossible to escape the working class.

All of these changes were significant, but something else shifted at this time, something truly momentous: Time began to equal money. Employees worked with machines that put out a relatively stable number of products per hour. So the longer the machine was running, the more product a factory would produce and the more money the owner could make. More hours meant more money.

Employees were usually paid not by the task, as they had been for centuries before, but by the hour. I've tried to imagine what it was like for a worker at that time when they collected their first week's wages after a lifetime of growing crops or tatting lace, but I find it difficult to conceive of a time when pay was unconnected to the hours invested. Not only was this metamorphosis recent, but it was rapid. It may have begun in England, but it soon spread across nations and even continents.

Even our vocabulary reflected this change. In the 1600s, for example, the word *punctuality* meant "exactness." Somewhere around 1777 or so, people began to use the word to mean "on time." For centuries, the word *efficiency* meant "the power to get something done," from the Latin verb *efficere,* which means "to accomplish." But in the 1780s, we see it used as a synonym for *productive work,* and in 1858, an article first used *efficiency* to mean "the ratio of useful work done to energy expended." *Time well spent* began to mean "time during which money was earned."

This transformation was not isolated to dusty factory floors, though; it extended even to our conception of the natural world. Whereas our schedules were once governed by the rising and falling of the sun, the very definition of *daytime* evolved, pulling focus away from the heavens and down to earth. Part of this was simply because more and more people could cut through the darkness with artificial light.

In 1834, Joseph Morgan developed a method for commercially producing candles. Light inside the home became generally affordable, and then candles became even more widely used in the 1850s after the invention of paraffin wax, which made them cleaner, more reliable, and cheaper. In 1879, Thomas Edison produced the first lightbulb that could be commercially manufactured and sold.

Night shifts became possible. Sundown was no longer quitting time. *Day* once meant "waking hours," during sunlight, but when daylight lost its significance, *day* came to mean "working hours." Workers could start their "days" before the sun rose, or end them long after nightfall.

In truth, we were not ready for the sudden changes spurred by the steam engine. When factories first started replacing farms, there were no laws governing labor practices and no regulations to protect workers. It was all too new. No politician anticipated a need to create oversight mechanisms or punish abuses. What's more, there was a heady excitement among government leaders as they saw factories go up and profit margins rise. Very few people wanted to erect barriers that might hinder progress. We're talking, of course, about the age leading up to the twentieth century, to the Roaring Twenties and the excesses depicted in *The Great Gatsby.* For industrialists, the freewheeling atmosphere in economics and government led to an orgy of profitable exploitation.

Because of the lax environment, the nineteenth century saw some of the worst abuses of paid laborers in human history. One of my favorite authors as a child was (and still as an adult) Charles Dickens. I read a biography of him while I was in fourth or fifth grade and was horrified to learn about what he endured.

Dickens never forgot his time working at a blacking warehouse when he was ten, the same age I was when I read of his early years. He earned six shillings a week to help pay his family's rent. The warehouse was a "crazy, tumble-down old house," Dickens told his friend John Forster, "literally overrun with rats. . . . My work was to cover the pots of paste-blacking; first with a piece of oil-paper, and then with a piece of blue paper; to tie them round with a string; and then to clip the paper close and neat, all round, until it looked as smart as a pot of ointment from an apothecary's shop. When a certain number of grosses of pots had attained this pitch of perfection, I was to paste on each a printed label, and then go on again with more pots."

Hundreds if not thousands of times, the child's small fingers draped the colored paper, wrapped the string, and trimmed the edges. Over and over, for hours on end. Based solely on the number of times that Dickens referred to this experience, we know it clearly had a monumental impact on him.

The economist Rick Bookstaber writes, "The Industrial Revolution ultimately increased prosperity, but for a time it made a wide swath of the populace worse off. The period of transition from the domestic to the factory system of industry and from the older to the new agriculture was one of almost unrelieved misery for those who could not integrate into the new economy, whether due to lack of capital or lack of physical or mental adaptability."

The period of transition that Bookstaber refers to lasted for decades. The age of "unrelieved misery" spanned at least a generation. Keep in mind that one of Charles Dickens's grandsons died in 1962. That's how recent this history is.

In the early industrial age, children worked either all day or all night—as one crawled into bed, another went to work. Here's the awful takeaway for me: It wasn't moral outrage that finally ended child labor, but the extreme rates of mortality among the young. Leaders were worried about the "physical preservation of the race."

There are whole books dedicated to describing the suffering of workers in the early days of the Industrial Revolution, but I'm mentioning these abuses here to illustrate how drastically working conditions were altered after mechanization. Not all the alterations were abusive, but many of them certainly were.

So how does this history connect to our lives in the twenty-first century? I didn't see the connection until I began to learn about the battles over hours and the accepted definition of a "reasonable" working day. Before the nineteenth century, people worked an average of six to eight hours a day and enjoyed dozens of days off throughout the year. In fact, even those in the lowest strata of society spent as much time at rest as they did at labor. Quite suddenly, people were expected to work punishing hours with no time off.

Thus, when labor unions began to form and to press for fewer hours, each worker was fighting not for new protections but, says James E. Thorold Rogers, "to recover what his ancestor worked by four or five centuries ago." In other words, people wanted to return to the same kind of working habits they had before moving to urban areas and large-scale production lines. Remember this: The fight over working hours has, from the start, been about returning to the kind of life we had for millennia.

In 1870, Sir John Lubbock was elected to Parliament. The first Baron of Avebury was a banker and a scientist (he coined the terms *paleolithic* and *neolithic* to describe the two Stone Ages), but he was also a fierce warrior for social justice and for the people he identified as the hardest working in the community.

Once elected, he began immediately pushing to enact some workers' protections. A year later, he got the Bank Holidays Act to set aside four days of the year as holidays. It was the first time in about a hundred years that workers were given time off for no religious or civic reason, but just to enjoy their leisure. Those days were commonly known as St. Lubbock's Days, in honor of the man who fought for them.

All around Europe and the United States at that time, workers were fighting for limited hours and better conditions. The push for an eight-hour workday was spearheaded by textile manufacturer Robert Owen, who wanted to create better conditions for his own factory employees. Owen created the now familiar motto: "Eight hours' labour, eight hours' recreation, eight hours' rest."

But most employers weren't ready to follow Owen's model and be satisfied with getting only eight hours of work from their employees. A law passed in 1847 forced them to work women and children in Britain for only ten hours a day. And similar legislation was passed in France, where employees were restricted to twelve hours.

This struggle was going on across the Atlantic as well. The Workingman's Party of the United States was founded in 1877, as was the Amalgamated Association of Iron, Steel, and Tin Workers and the Brotherhood of Locomotive Engineers (although women made up a sizable portion of the workforce, most of the early labor unions were exclusively male). Tens of thousands marched in the first Labor Day parade in New York in September 1882. What were they marching for? Limits to working hours.

The response to these efforts among the upper class was mostly derisive and sometimes dangerously aggressive. Strikes were quelled with force by police and the military. While this may seem like ancient history, these clashes occurred during our great-grandparents' time, and they laid the groundwork for today's relationships between employers and workers.

One of the most well known of these confrontations occurred in Chicago in 1886, at a rally in support of workers' rights that was intended to be peaceful. At that time, some were earning only $1.50 a day, working sixty hours a week. The working class saw the lavish homes and lifestyles enjoyed by factory owners, and their patience ran out. Membership in the Knights of Labor, which advocated for an eight-hour day, swelled from 70,000 to more than 700,000 in just two years.

Hundreds met in Chicago's Haymarket Square to, as the labor activist August Spies said, "explain the general situation of the eight-hour movement." Early on, though, a homemade bomb was thrown at advancing police. The explosion killed an officer and ignited chaos. When the smoke and crowds cleared, seven officers had been killed, along with several civilians, and dozens of people were wounded. While this event was a tragedy, violence like this was common whenever workers pushed for reform.

Still, labor protection started gaining political support as the nineteenth century gave way to the twentieth. The first nation to establish the eight-hour workday was Uruguay, in

1915, just a year after that country's president instituted unemployment compensation policies.

In August 1919, Dr. Stephen Bauer opened his article in the *Monthly Labor Review* this way: "In the last months of the year 1918 the eight-hour day has become the war cry of the masses; the employers retort that it can be introduced only by international action. Thus, there arise once more the questions as to the reasons which determine the duration of the hours of labor, the effects of their shortening, and the most efficient methods of their regulation."

Consider for just a moment how painfully our ancestors suffered and how hard they worked to secure fewer working hours for themselves and their children. Today, less than a hundred years later, we've ceded that ground almost without a fight. We choose to work long hours and answer work texts because we think it's the only way to keep our jobs or do them well. But it has not always been like this. Our habits can change because it hasn't been all that long since we started following them.

How did we get from hunger strikes and fistfights with police officers to voluntarily answering emails on Sunday night and choosing to stay in the office to "finish up"? In the book *The Jobless Future,* Stanley Aronowitz and William DiFazio bemoan this trend, writing, "An alarming number of workers, both intellectual and manual, surrender nearly all their waking and even dreaming hours to labor. . . . The notion of free time is as distant from most people's everyday experience as open space."

Yet we've known for more than a hundred years that long hours of toil don't actually increase productivity. We have data on this going back to the 1800s—at the time when unions forced employers to cut hours, factory owners were surprised to find that productivity increased while accidents decreased. Overwork was counterproductive in the days of the sweatshop, and research shows it still is, even in the age of the knowledge worker.

This isn't just about working hours, of course. It's no surprise that employers will try to get as many hours as they can from their workers and employees will often put in extra time voluntarily in order to earn promotions or raises. That's understandable. But we are where we are now because of what happened *after* the victory over working hours. When employers lost the political fight, they moved to a new field of battle: culture.

Chapter 3

WORK ETHIC

> Idleness so called, which does not consist in doing nothing, but in doing a great deal not recognized in the dogmatic formularies of the ruling class, has as good a right to state its position as industry itself.
>
> —ROBERT LOUIS STEVENSON, *"An Apology for Idlers," 1877*

JUST AS THERE WERE many economic and technological ideas brewing for centuries before they helped give birth to the industrial age, there were philosophies as well—most important, the Protestant work ethic. Martin Luther didn't just change religious history when he nailed his Ninety-Five Theses to the church doors of Wittenburg, Germany. His ideas eventually changed the lives of nearly every person in the developed world.

For a long time, the Catholic Church taught that believers must perform good works in order to attain heaven. Remember that sloth (a reluctance to work) is one of the seven deadly sins. Catholic priests quoted from the Epistle of James: "Show me your faith without deeds and I will show you my faith *by my deeds* [emphasis added]." Luther despised the practice of allowing people to buy salvation through gifts to charity, so he emphasized hard work and frugality instead.

Though Luther argued that salvation was achieved through faith alone, he also taught that hard work is a gift of God and that we can recognize good and faithful people through the hard work they do and their efficient labor. Luther believed that idleness should be enjoyed only *after* death.

All of this might have remained within the walls of the church and the homes of the faithful were it not for Max Weber. In 1904, just as labor unions were gaining strength and the push for eight-hour workdays was gaining ground, the German sociologist published a book called *The Protestant Ethic and the Spirit of Capitalism*. Weber's description of what Luther believed wasn't wholly accurate, but his economic argument was hugely influential.

Weber argued that the Protestant work ethic was largely responsible for the growth of capitalism and the success of northern Europe. In the book, he quotes Benjamin Franklin's now famous advice: "Remember that *time* is money. He that can earn ten shillings a day by his labour, and goes abroad, or sits idle one half of that day, though he spends but sixpence during his diversion or idleness, ought not to reckon *that* the only expense; he hath really spent or thrown away five shillings besides." Translation: If you sit around, you aren't just lazy—you are also wasting money.

Max Weber points out that before the industrial age, farmworkers who were offered a higher wage would work fewer hours. They would work long enough to earn what they needed and then spend their extra time at leisure. The Protestant work ethic, though, viewed idleness as immoral and hard work as virtuous. So employers could convince devout employees to work long hours regardless of the wages paid. Even the janitor and the plumber are doing God's work, according to Martin Luther, and no job is unworthy in the eyes of the Lord.

Weber's book was very popular and had an outsize impact on economic policies. In fact, the International Sociological Association named it the fourth most important twentieth-century book in the field.

The idolization of hardworking people began in the United States with good old Ben Franklin and the like-minded. It grew in strength during the nineteenth century. In 1859, Frederick Douglass first gave a speech that he would repeat multiple times in the ensuing years. It was a lecture on the "self-made man." "There is nothing good, great, or desirable," he said, "that does not come by some kind of labor."

This vision of a man (let's be honest: it was almost always a man at that time) who achieved great things solely through toil and grit became an essential part of the American Dream, and some version of it took hold in many parts of Europe as well. "My theory of self-made men is, then, simply this: that they are men of work," Douglass said. "Whether or not such men have acquired material, moral or intellectual excellence, honest labor faithfully, steadily and persistently pursued, is the best, if not the only, explanation of their success."

His argument is that the success of someone who achieves great things is mostly due to blood, sweat, and tears. Conversely, someone who is unsuccessful is obviously not working hard enough.

Once again, we see the changes in the language that reflect

an evolution in philosophy. For example, the word *bootstrapping* was originally used in the early 1800s. It meant "to pull yourself over a fence using only your bootstraps"; in other words, doing something ridiculously improbable. An article in the *Madison City Express* from 1843 mocked an official by saying, "His Excellency is certainly attempting to lift himself up by his boot-straps, or, what is much better, is 'sitting in a wheelbarrow to wheel himself.' "

In the ensuing decades, the satirical implications were lost and the word came to mean going from rags to riches through only individual effort. It became a compliment. This mirrored the opinions of a broader society that, both in the United States and in much of Europe, admired not the idle rich but self-made men like Thomas Edison and Henry Ford.

Enter Horatio Alger. Alger was the son of a Unitarian minister who struggled with money for most of his life. The young man secured a place at Harvard, but his humble background kept him from entering the elite clubs there. That may have been part of his inspiration for the novels he eventually became famous for.

Horatio Alger's first commercially successful book was called *Ragged Dick*. Telling the story of a poor fourteen-year-old shoeshine boy who rises in life because of his honesty, frugality, and bravery, the book was a blockbuster. Alger wrote basically the same story for the rest of his life and simply changed the characters and other superficial details. Today, if someone mentions a "Horatio Alger story," they mean a rags-to-riches tale in which a plucky young hero achieves success through his own good character and hard work.

Alger's novels were so popular and so integral to American

culture between 1867 and 1926 that his mythical tales became something to emulate. It was no longer ludicrous to try to pull oneself up by one's bootstraps; it was a solid life plan. Even today, despite the income gap being higher in the United States than in almost any other nation, many Americans believe they can rise to riches through honest labor, and that belief fuels a willingness to work too much, even when we're not reaping the profits of our labor.

The psychologists Michael W. Kraus and Jacinth J. X. Tan studied American views on social mobility for a paper published in 2015. They concluded, "Beliefs in the American Dream permeate our parenting decisions, educational practices, and political agendas, and yet, according to data we present in this manuscript, Americans are largely inaccurate when asked to describe actual trends in social class mobility in society."

Inaccurate is a mild word to use here. In truth, your chances of becoming a millionaire in the United States are less than one percent. The likelihood that you'll become a billionaire is about the same as the chance that you'll be struck by lightning. But we are not very accurate even when gauging less dramatic changes in income. Kraus and Tan reported that participants in four studies vastly overestimated the possibility that someone could move from low income to high income.

A separate study from Princeton revealed that the stronger your belief that you can rise through the income ranks, the more likely you are to defend the status quo. If you think your life could be a Horatio Alger story, you're more likely to support the existing economic and political policies instead of pushing for change. *Never mind that most of my friends and neighbors earn as much now as they did ten years ago,* many think to themselves. *I'll be the exception.* I used to tell prospective employers during interviews that though I may have had less experience than other applicants, I could "work anyone under the table."

While an obsession with efficiency and productivity is found all over the world, nowhere is it more evident than in the United States, where nearly 70 percent of citizens believe they will achieve the American Dream and that the most important factors in achieving economic success are hard work and personal drive.

John Swansburg, senior editor of the *Atlantic,* wrote about his father's pursuit of the American Dream and the myth of the self-made man (and woman) and ultimately asks an important question: "Is it a healthy myth that inspires us to aim high? Or is it more like a mass delusion keeping us from confronting the fact that poor Americans tend to remain poor Americans, regardless of how hard they work?" I tend to think it is more mass delusion than healthy myth, especially since as a younger person I fervently believed that someone somewhere would eventually recognize how hard I worked and reward me. I ultimately had to recognize my efforts and reward myself.

This belief in hard work as a virtue and a life philosophy started on the door of a church in Germany. Over the course of a couple hundred years, the religious notion that working long and hard makes you deserving while taking time off makes you lazy was adopted as an economic policy, a way to motivate employees and get the most out of them.

In the end, this story is about how the industrialist desire to have fewer workers doing more hours of work merged with the religious belief that work is good and idleness is bad, along with a capitalist faith in constant growth. When time became money, the need to get more time out of workers became urgent if profit targets were to be met.

It's interesting to note that the man who helped create the belief in long hours and productivity, Max Weber, expressed some doubts in the conclusion of his popular book. After asserting, "When asceticism was carried out of monastic cells into everyday life . . . it did its part in building the tremendous cosmos of the modern economic order," he wrote that machinery had come to control the lives of most people, and he wondered if it would continue to determine their lives "until the last ton of fossilized coal is burnt" and the industry that was meant to improve human life would ultimately become "an iron cage." His concern that we would exhaust our resources and imprison ourselves has been justified. Yet even as we see the disastrous effects of past policies, we're still told to keep working, just as our parents and grandparents were told.

It was common, in the early twentieth century, for writers to berate people for their indolence. John Candee Dean wrote a piece for the *Indianapolis Star* in 1920 in which he said, "After you have worked six, eight, ten or even twelve hours day, do not think your remaining hours can be wasted in pleasure. . . . Do not waste your time at the 'movies,' at the theater or in the street. If you will employ all your spare time well, you can not only become financially independent, but also a man of education."

Work was merging with identity at this time. No more dilettantes studying archaeology while working as a banker and a novelist—the industrial age saw the ascendancy of engineers, inventors, and entrepreneurs like Henry Ford. Ford was world renowned for his work ethic, and an excerpt from his autobiography reads more like a sermon than a treatise on industry. "Work is our sanity," Ford wrote. "Our self-respect, our salvation. Through work and work alone may health, wealth, and happiness be secured."

The transformation this idea caused in the world at large cannot be overestimated. When time is money, idle hours are a waste of money. This is the philosophical underpinning of all our modern stress: that time is too valuable to waste. We don't pass time, we spend it. It's no wonder that we don't really have pastimes anymore.

When work is what makes someone worthwhile and deserving, those who don't work as much as possible are seen as undeserving and worthless. To many in Henry Ford's time, it was more shameful to miss a day at work than to stay home from church. I would argue that work began to replace religion. In fact, experts predict that by 2035 those with no religious affiliation will outnumber Protestants in the United States. So the faith declines, but the work ethic it created remains.

Almost as soon as the eight-hour workday was accepted as standard, workers began to voluntarily work longer days in order to rise through the ranks and earn the admiration of coworkers and managers. "Our society measures personal worth in terms of productivity, efficiency, and the maximization of our potential," the Calvin College philosophy professor Rebecca Konyndyk DeYoung writes. "So we'd better get busy or we'll be good for nothing."

It's clear, though, that the average worker hadn't fully bought into this story line by the early twentieth century. My grandparents were still "wasting their time" gardening and going to social clubs and spending hours in national parks enjoying the view without taking pictures to share on Instagram. It would take another fifty or sixty years for most of us to believe the company line. Still, this underlying faith in productivity, hard work, and efficiency was bubbling beneath the surface when the world went to war. At that point, efficient production became not just a goal but a necessity, in order to support the war effort.

After World War I ended in 1918, there was a reconsideration of labor and productivity among economists. If anything, the allure of the American Dream grew stronger. Not even the Great Depression dimmed the optimism of John Maynard Keynes, the most influential economist of the twentieth century. His famous essay from 1930, "Economic Possibilities for Our Grandchildren," predicted that the Depression was a blip on the financial radar screen, temporary and soon forgotten.

Keynes predicted that by 2030, people would work only fifteen hours a week and that would be enough to keep everyone fed, clothed, and housed. "For the first time since his creation," Keynes wrote, "man will be faced with his real, his permanent problem—how to use his freedom from pressing economic cares, how to occupy the leisure, which science and compound interest will have won."

Keynes was not correct in his predictions, but there was nothing wrong with the great economist's math. He saw how quickly technology was advancing and he added that to productivity gains and compounding interest and saw that the developed world could eventually produce the same amount of wealth in far fewer hours. Keynes's vision for the future should have been accurate. So why was he so wrong?

As the Georgetown economist Karl Widerquist said, "This prediction is not so much an error as a puzzle: how can the one plus one so correctly predicted by Keynes have failed to equal two? . . . It didn't seem logical to people in 1930 that the economy could continue to grow without freeing us from the struggle for survival." And it doesn't seem logical to me either, nearly ninety years after Keynes's predictions.

How is it that we produce so much wealth with our labor and yet most of us feel we are barely hanging on to our standard of living, let alone creating a situation in which our children will do better than we've done? Why do I have more to do than my grandmother, despite owning a dishwasher, microwave, and portable computer?

The answer can be found in the decades between the end of World War II and 1980. Keynes was right about at least one thing: The Great Depression was just a temporary lull for the driving engine of the Industrial Revolution. When warplanes began to roll off the factory lines in the 1940s and tens of thousands of women went to work to replace the men who'd been called to service, it was like a defibrillator charge to the stuttering heart of capitalism.

The process of supplying and carrying out military operations on a global scale taught Europe and the United States that the manufacturing industry could be incredibly productive with a much smaller number of workers than previously employed. Although citizens were limited by ration systems, losing a colossal percentage of the male workforce to the military didn't cripple economies or slow productivity.

The battle over hours seemed settled at that point. The division of the day into blocks of eight (eight for work, eight for sleep, eight for leisure) seemed firmly established in the years after World War II. As Juliet Schor writes in *The Overworked American,* "By the late 1950s, the problem of excessive working hours had been solved—at least in the minds of experts. The four-day week was thought to 'loom on the immediate horizon.'"

You see, Keynes wasn't the only person who thought working hours would soon shrink significantly. The evolutionary biologist Julian Huxley believed people would get five days off "when we reach the point when the world produces all the goods that it needs in two days." At that point, Huxley said, "We must curtail our production of goods and turn our attention to the great problem of what to do with our new leisure."

In 1965, a Senate subcommittee predicted that by the year 2000, Americans would work fourteen-hour weeks and take nearly two months of vacation time. Instead, the average American gets ten days of paid vacation and nearly one in four gets no paid holidays at all. Sadly, two things occurred that prevented a drop in working hours: a rise in consumerism and a steep rise in income inequality.

First, many workers started using their extra income not to work less but to buy more. Because the economy is dependent on growth, officials told the populace, it is patriotic to buy more things. Marketing became a major industry, creating a desire for things that were unnecessary but attractive. The success of Christmas seemed contingent on the amount consumers spent on buying gifts.

Another reason many of us now define ourselves by our job titles is pay scale. In order for all workers to benefit from a rise in profits, all workers would have to get a reasonable portion of those profits. Instead, between the 1960s and today, worker pay has stagnated or grown slowly (when adjusted for inflation), whereas CEO pay has skyrocketed. The profits that Keynes thought would fund a more leisurely lifestyle for all have mostly gone to a tiny percentage of the population.

While the costs of goods went down for everyone, the profit from the sale of those goods has gone to a fraction of the populace. "The benefits of productivity were not shared equally," says the historian Nelson Lichtenstein, director of the Center for the Study of Work, Labor, and Democracy. Many of the companies that have revolutionized retail sales were founded decades ago. Walmart, for example, first opened its doors in July 1962.

"One of the great things about Walmart," Lichtenstein told me, "is that productivity in retail increased dramatically, but the benefits were not shared with workers. Income inequality is a function of power inequality. That gap is a function of the power differential." The United States has more private wealth than any other nation in the world, for example, but the fourth highest gap between rich and poor of any country studied by the Organisation for Economic Cooperation and Development (OECD).

This is partly why so many people feel they are working an incredible number of hours without making progress financially: The benefits of their hard work are accruing in someone else's account. According to data from the Economic Policy Institute, pay for non-management workers increased by less than 12 percent between 1978 and 2016. On the other hand, CEO pay jumped by more than 800 percent if you include stock options.

We marvel at the luxury enjoyed by English dukes and German barons of bygone eras, but the top earners now live more lavishly than the Crawley family in *Downton Abbey*. The only difference is the income gap is *wider* today between CEOs and their workers than it was between the fictional Earl of Grantham and his valet.

So, after the industrial age took hold, workers put in more hours, became less likely to own their tools, and were less invested in the end product than they had been at the dawn of the nineteenth century. Also, the Calvinistic belief that work is virtuous and idleness is sin had been transformed into a faith in capitalism to reward those who worked the hardest and the longest.

In the United States, the World War II generation (the so-called Greatest Generation) believed anyone could achieve success. The political analyst Jared Yates Sexton says, "The Greatest Generation thought if they couldn't become successful, they could at least prove they tried. So success became almost less important than how hard you worked." There was a sense that working as hard as you could was your duty as a citizen.

The workplace started to resemble the home, with kitchens and lunchrooms and social areas, so there was less reason to leave the office. All of these small changes slowly accumulated. Until the 1970s, Americans put in the same number of hours at work as most Europeans and fewer than the French, but that isn't true anymore.

People became used to the habits of the workplace—staying busy, competing with coworkers, constantly searching for improvements in efficiency—and they began to take those habits home. In America, the United Kingdom, and Australia especially, people began to notice how much time they spent at home on seemingly worthless activities. They began to feel they didn't have time to waste on board games and coin collecting.

The Nobel Prize–winning economist Gary S. Becker wrote in 1965: "If anything, time is used more carefully today than a century ago. When people are paid more, they work longer hours because work is so much more profitable than leisure." Now the average American works 140 hours more per year than the average British citizen and 300 hours more than the average worker in France. We are trading leisure time for money, and because wages haven't grown much, the trade isn't a good one.

The sense that time was too valuable to be spent at a barbecue or baseball game started to make people feel anxious about what they did in their off-hours. Leisure began to feel stressful. In the back of their minds, people worried about the money they weren't making.

This trend toward using every minute profitably had been strengthening for centuries by the time the 1970s came to a close. Yet some kind of balance had been maintained between work hours and free time; a shaky but real separation existed between the habits of the office and the habits in the home.

That balance was about to be lost.

Chapter 4

TIME BECOMES MONEY

It's ironic that they give you a watch, isn't it?

—JARED YATES SEXTON

I USED TO CREATE elaborate story tapes for my friends for which I wrote semibiographical tales about our lives, then inserted bits of music to illustrate the story. One Christmas, I wrote a poem about Santa Claus wanting to quit because he felt the world was too cynical. It took weeks to complete the project, but in the end, all of my friends received a holiday card and a fully produced narrated story with sound effects and movie clips and lots of music.

I also used to write poetry and plays and create elaborate scrapbooks, take dance classes, and make my own embroidered towels, in addition to working full-time, taking voice lessons, and performing in professional productions of opera and musical theater. I look back now and wonder how in the hell I had the time. I was broke back then, and scraping to pay every bill.

Honestly, it feels like the more money I earn, the less time I have. As it turns out, that is not just my problem. Over the past twenty or thirty years, the people who used to work all the time (the lower earners) are now the ones with more time to spare, while upper income brackets are overscheduled.

If this lack of time were all about the workplace, then my difficulties would have disappeared when I left the office environment for good. If it were a problem with corporate expectations, then my issues would have ended when I resigned in 2018. And yet, instead of having time to spare, I found I was busier as a business owner than as an employee. How did that make sense?

In the end, it all comes down to time: our relationship with it, our understanding of it, the value we put on it. Before the industrial age, time was measured in days or seasons. However, when workers began punching in and out of work, our understanding of time changed, as did our enjoyment of our time off.

Consider for a moment this experiment run by Sanford DeVoe and Julian House of UCLA and the University of Toronto, respectively. DeVoe and House split their study participants into two groups. Both groups listened to the first eighty-six seconds of the lushly beautiful "Flower Duet" from an opera by Leo Délibes. If you've never heard it, find a recording and listen with your eyes closed. It's an exquisite piece of music with the soprano and mezzo voices entangled in close harmony and a leap to a high B in the middle that never fails to give me goose bumps.

The lyrics read, in part, "Underneath the dome, the jasmine comes to greet the roses, by the flower banks, fresh and bright. Come, and we'll join them. We'll glide with the tide, on we'll ride away through little shimmering waves, rowing lightly and carelessly." Délibes created a ravishing melodic line that perfectly reflects the poetry.

Participants in the study had to fill out short questionnaires. Before they started listening, one group was asked to estimate their hourly wage. That group, the one that had been forced to think about how much their time is worth, was much more impatient for the music to end. Remember, they heard less than a minute and a half of stunningly gorgeous music. But, as DeVoe says, "they wanted to get to the end of the experiment to do something that was more profitable."

What those study participants felt was time scarcity. As something rises in value, it begins to seem rarer and more precious. So you can feel as though you're short on time, even if you're not. Only your perception has changed.

This overriding sense that time is scarce and expensive was born when our earnings became dependent on the number of hours we worked. "Ever since a clock was first used to synchronise labour in the eighteenth century," said the *Economist* in December 2014, "time has been understood in relation to money. Once hours are financially quantified, people worry more about wasting, saving or using them profitably. When economies grow and incomes rise, everyone's time becomes more valuable. And the more valuable something becomes, the scarcer it seems." Translation: The more money you make, the more likely you'll believe that you have no time to waste. This helps explain why I felt more overwhelmed as my income rose.

Here's the truth: Most of us are *not* working more hours than we were ten to twenty years ago. In fact, we're working fewer hours, on average. Surprised? Let me explain.

The trend of feeling overwhelmed despite less work began some twenty years ago. As Gallup pointed out in a 2011 report, "The more cash-rich working Americans are, the more time-poor they feel." The reality is, when it comes to sheer number of hours worked, the United States does not top the list. In a ranking of average weekly work hours, America comes in at number 14. Mexico, Costa Rica, South Korea, and Greece all work about forty hours or more. Americans work about thirty-four. (Remember, that's an average of all workers, including those working part-time.)

Americans are not the only ones feeling this increased pressure, despite working fewer hours. A number of agencies in Europe are studying work-related stress caused by, among other things, "heavy workload" and "long working hours." Nearly a quarter of European workers say they suffer from stress related to their jobs, and one in five Brits told researchers they felt their life was out of control. And yet despite the complaints about long hours, full-time workers in Switzerland, Italy, Belgium, and France work twenty to thirty hours *less* each week than workers in the nineteenth century.

If you examine all the surveys based on *self-reporting,* that is, asking people what they do with their time, you'll get the sense that everyone is working almost all the time. The productivity expert Laura Vanderkam heard from many women that they worked sixty hours a week on average. But when she had them keep time logs, she found they actually worked about forty-four hours a week.

Daniel Hamermesh of the University of Texas calls this phenomenon "yuppie kvetch" (*kvetch* is a Yiddish term for a complainer), but I think the derogatory implication of that phrase is unfair and here's why: More than half of U.S. employees *feel* overworked or overwhelmed on a regular basis, according to a study from the Families and Work Institute. The president of this nonprofit research center, Ellen Galinsky, told ABC News that "many American employees are near the breaking point." I really doubt that all of those people are imagining their stress so they have something to complain about. I believe they really feel that way because *I feel that way too.*

Nearly one in four people tell researchers that they get only one day off, or work every day. Studies done by the payroll services company Paychex show most workers feel stressed three or more days every week. Research from the National Institute for Occupational Safety and Health shows that about 40 percent of workers feel "overworked, pressured, and squeezed to the point of anxiety, depression, and disease."

Regardless of how much people are actually working, the stress these people feel is very real and should be taken seriously. Stress is both dangerous to one's health and, in a business sense, expensive. I first began to rethink my habits after I got severely ill twice in less than five months, and ended up spending a total of fourteen days in bed and even more days at work feeling horrible while my body tried to recover.

The American Institute of Stress says more than half of all doctor visits are prompted by stress-related illness. By some estimates, businesses in the United States alone lose more than $300 billion every year because of absenteeism and health-care costs related to stress and anxiety. If you note that at least 25 percent of Europeans are suffering the same symptoms, you can begin to understand the magnitude of this global problem.

Here's another mathematical nuance to this picture: Though we are working fewer hours now than we were in the past, it's unclear exactly how wide that gap is. While the data seem to indicate that many people vastly overestimate the number of hours they work, the truth is, it's quite difficult to get an accurate measure of people's working hours. We don't really know for sure how much people are working at this point in history because work life and home life are so thickly entangled.

We bring our work home with us now, answering emails at nine p.m. and picking up the phone when we're out to dinner. That's why I don't have time for story tapes and dance classes anymore. But the leakage flows both ways. We also do a significant amount of nonwork activities while we're at work. We book airline tickets and order new shoes and make dinner reservations and send notes to our relatives. If you spend a couple hours every day doing online shopping, should statisticians subtract that time from your total work hours, and then add in the time you spent writing a note to a coworker from your dinner table?

Research from Roland Paulsen at Lund University showed that employees spend about half of their workday "cyberslacking," or engaged in nonwork activities not related to their primary job responsibilities. More than half of all online purchases are transacted between nine a.m. and five p.m., and almost two-thirds of the traffic at porn sites occurs during the workday. Few jobs legitimately involve the viewing of pornographic videos, so I think it's safe to assume we can include that in "nonwork activities."

Certainly, the line between home and office has blurred, and you could argue many of us are never truly off the job. It's easy to see that most people around the globe are experiencing what the Australia Institute, a think tank based in Canberra, calls "polluted time." This is a phenomenon caused by having to handle work duties during off-hours, being on call, or even having to think carefully about work issues or problem-solving while technically not on the job.

"Polluted time," writes Josh Fear, the deputy director of the institute, "is one of the many consequences of a labour market which has become increasingly 'flexible' over the past few decades. All too often the benefits of such flexibility have flowed to employers." In this case, "flexibility" means that you won't be fired (in most cases) for answering a call from your spouse while you're on the job, but you're also expected to immediately answer an email from your boss at ten a.m. on a Saturday. I'm sure it comes as no surprise that the most common task carried out during off-hours is reading and answering email.

So, ask yourself a question, the same question I've had to ask myself: Are you happy with the balance between your worklife and your personal life? Do you regularly spend time doing things unrelated to work without thinking about work or feeling the need to check your inbox? Not thinking about your job is crucial, because every time you click that envelope icon, you are "polluting your time."

With work intruding on our home life and home life encroaching on work hours, many people now never have a sense of being completely separate from their jobs. It's as though we are now on twenty-four-hour call. That can be incredibly hard on the both the body and the mind and it explains why people feel they're working more hours. They may feel they never truly punch out of work. When you ask how many hours they are working, it's possible they only report those hours spent in the office.

I don't think the statistics on how many hours people work give us the full picture of the modern workload. Those feelings people are experiencing of being overworked and stressed are real. And the impact of all that stress on people's health and well-being can be disastrous.

Even if people seek treatment for stress-related disorders connected to their work habits, they are often reluctant to cut their hours or stop working during their off-time. My doctor told me to take time off and I fully intended to do so, but I didn't end up changing my habits one iota. Many of us think we have to be on call all the time in order to keep our jobs, and that assumption may be reinforced by company policy and messaging from executives.

Yet the idea that long hours are good for business is at least a half-century outdated. Perhaps Bob Cratchit needed to put in fourteen hours a day in order to record all of Scrooge's financial transactions, but he could probably get all that done in a couple of hours using today's technology and be on his way home to play with his kids. (Plus, it's likely that Tiny Tim's ailment was treatable and could have been cured with regular gulps of modern vitamin D–fortified milk.)

Advances in computing and communication tools mean it takes much less time to do many jobs, and yet we're still stuck slogging away for hours on end as though the Digital Revolution never happened. Corporate management still has a nineteenth-century mind-set in a twenty-first-century workplace.

This state of affairs is partly explained by Parkinson's Law: "Work expands so as to fill the time available for its completion."

That's not a scientific principle but an adage first expressed by the historian Cyril Northcote.

That means when we are contracted to work eight hours a day but only have five hours' worth of work, we'll stretch out the tasks in order to make them fill the time available, like a cubic foot of nitrogen expanding to fill an entire house. We'll hold meetings and discuss trivial issues and send email and create agendas and add complexities until we need a full forty hours a week to do twenty-five hours' worth of work.

While it's true in theory that employers appreciate getting things done quickly, they often do not in practice. Keep in mind the "time is money" principle. It's incredibly difficult to evaluate a worker based on subjective measures like quality, innovation, or creative problem-solving. But it's simple and easy to record how many hours a worker spends on the job and whether tasks are completed on time. Quality of work is rarely measurable, but hours of work are.

When time became an acceptable currency, it also became common to pay people and reward them according to how many hours they worked. If you're assigned a project by your boss, you're probably better off inflating the estimate of how hard it will be and how long it will take. If your boss sees you laboring on it for weeks, they're more likely to be impressed when you complete it than if you zipped through it in a couple of days. (I'm not advocating deception in your work habits, by the way, but simply pointing out how illogical the current system is.)

Having to spend eight hours at work no matter how much time your actual job requires leads people to shop online and make doctor's appointments and generally take care of personal duties while technically on the clock. If you don't get home until after many workplaces are closed, how else are you supposed to get these things done? For most people, there is no spouse at home taking care of personal tasks while we focus solely on work. The system demands that we bring our home lives into our offices, and vice versa.

For the most part, the seeping of work into the home was intentionally instigated by managers and employers in the decades between World War II and 2010. So let's pick up our historical timeline in the year 1980.

A quick reminder of what was happening at that time: The Iran-Iraq War began with an invasion in September, Ronald Reagan was elected president of the United States in November, and John Lennon was shot and killed in December. Reagan's counterpart in the United Kingdom was Margaret Thatcher, who had become prime minister the previous spring.

During the Reagan/Thatcher era, the working world was transformed once more, not as extensively as was seen during the Industrial Revolution, but through an aggressive heightening of the attitudes toward labor that had been evolving for more than a hundred years. The United States began to follow policies based on so-called trickle-down economics: the idea that growth in income and wealth for the highest earners in a society will also help the poor and middle class because the money will "trickle down" from the top.

This was also the era during which the belief in constant growth really took hold. The health of national economies was measured in terms of GDP (gross domestic product), and the value of a stock was often heavily based on forecasts of profit growth instead of stability or resilience. It was not enough for corporations to meet expectations. Investors wanted companies to beat projections.

An economy built around constant growth, though, may not be sustainable in the long run, and many economists have started to question economic policies that are based on a belief in unending increases. This issue has actually become a bone of contention among many who watch financial markets. Journalist and author Christopher Ketcham calls the dream of constant growth the "unifying faith of industrial civilization."

While there's no reason why incomes shouldn't continue to grow and, therefore, why the amount people are willing to pay for products would not also increase, the number of resources available to make those products is finite. I'm certainly not going to settle this issue in these pages, as economics is not an exact science and there may be no definitive answers. As the old joke goes, if you put ten economists into a room, you'll end up with eleven opinions. I'm only interested in this debate because of the impact it has on our working lives.

Graeme Maxton, secretary general of the Club of Rome and author of *The End of Progress*, tells me, "We have this 'common sense' belief that we need economic growth to create jobs and reduce inequality, that economic growth is the key to everything." Maxton says this is the reason the income gap is now wider in many places than it was two hundred years ago. Every time profits fell, fear led executives to take drastic steps, like cutting jobs and demanding longer shifts from the remaining staff. And global events have sparked that fear again and again.

Many industrialized nations endured incredible financial upheaval during the 1980s. Consider this: Since World War II, there have been four global recessions. Three of them occurred between 1975 and 1991. Historically, recessions often result in significant changes in the relationship between employer and employee.

When a recession hits and profits fall, many companies will immediately make cuts to staffing. The workers who keep their jobs are often called upon to pick up the tasks and duties left behind by laid-off employees, and it's unlikely the survivors will complain about the increase in workload because they're afraid they'll be laid off too. It's true that weekly hours haven't increased all that much in recent years, but time on the job has risen dramatically if you look at it on an annual basis.

Americans added almost a full week of work to their year during the 1990s. Days off disappeared and fewer vacations were taken in the aftermath of multiple recessions.

And the sad footnote to all of this is that people are sacrificing their personal lives to no tangible end. Longer hours do not usually mean more income. According to data from the U.S. Census Bureau, had the average income risen at the same rate as the overall economy, most households in the United States would bring in about $92,000 right now, not $50,000.

Yet the idea persisted that we could all jump into that top echelon of wealth if we only worked hard enough, or that we could protect our jobs by proving we deserve them. That's why working hours started climbing in the years just before 1970. For most people, leisure time fell by about a third in that time period. The sociologist Juliet Schor noted that people spent more time working and less time sleeping and eating. Fast food consumption rose. "Parents are devoting less attention to their children," Schor wrote in *The Overworked American*. "Stress is on the rise, partly owing to the 'balancing act' of reconciling the demands of work and family life."

Of course, all of this applies mostly to people working full-time. Because of repeated recessions and mass layoffs, the past forty years have seen a growing number of people join the ranks of the unemployed, the underemployed, and the self-employed. As the labor historian Nelson Lichtenstein explained to me, most self-employment is involuntary.

People usually work for themselves because they can't find a suitable position at a company or institution or they are cobbling together a living with multiple freelance jobs. I am an anomaly in that I chose self-employment. I work for myself because I can, and because my life was spinning out of control while I was working for someone else. As my own boss, I can, at a minimum, order myself to take some time off.

Now, one might think that an increase in work hours would bring a commensurate rise in productivity, if more time on the job always meant more work completed. For some time, that's exactly what happened. Worldwide, productivity rose in most countries during the 1990s and early 2000s.

Consider this: When productivity rises, companies can choose to produce more or work fewer hours. It's no surprise most companies have chosen the former. Technology has advanced so quickly that at this point most of us could have the same standard of living as our grandparents while working only half the year. "We actually could have chosen the four-hour day," Juliet Schor writes. "Or a working year of six months. Or, *every worker in the United States could now be taking every other year off from work—with pay* [emphasis is Schor's]."

Stop for just a moment and imagine what life might look like if you worked every other year. What would you do with your time? If you could spend 365 days in a row not getting up to go to work or answering emails, and not worry about losing your position or opportunities for advancement, how would you spend your days?

Sadly, we're not usually allowed to choose what to do with the benefits of increased productivity. Most of us have no say in how companies spend the growing profits earned by our labor. It's generally the CEO or board of directors who make that decision, and the increases are often seen in stockholder dividends or bonuses for executives.

The rest of us stay on the job for the full forty hours because that's what we're paid for and we'll often stay longer, even if we don't earn overtime, because that's what is demanded of us by managers who don't fully understand how to drive productivity or take advantage of its rewards.

So society was already fully committed to the worship of hard work during the 1980s and '90s, when a revolution occurred that really cemented the dominance of the myth of the self-made man: the rise of the tech billionaire.

Microsoft was founded in 1975, Apple one year later. Amazon started in 1994, Yahoo! in 1995, and Google in 1998. Those companies are massive now, but they mostly started with a couple guys working hard on a new kind of software, laboring away in virtual obscurity until their products became big sellers.

Back when Microsoft's revenue was only $1,600 a year, Bill Gates said he got up at four a.m. every day, worked sixteen hours, and sometimes spent the night in his office. Steve Jobs wouldn't get to his office at Apple until nine a.m., he told *Time,* but that was after working for an hour or two at home.

It seemed to the watching public that the most successful people were all slaving away on the computer from dawn until dusk, and sometimes longer. The entrepreneur Mark Cuban says he didn't take a vacation for seven years when he was starting out. Jeff Bezos and his colleagues at Amazon say they logged twelve-hour days, seven days a week in the mid-1990s, and Marissa Mayer reportedly worked 130 hours every week while she was at Google. This list could go on and on.

One of the most common adjectives used to describe the modern rock-star CEO is *workaholic.* It's usually intended as a compliment or sign of respect. "If you find yourself about to hit the snooze button again," Max Nisen wrote in *Business Insider,* "look [at these executives] for inspiration." Anim Aweh, a counselor whose practice is located near Silicon Valley in California, told the *New York Times,* "Everyone wants to be a model employee. One woman told me: 'The expectation is not that you should work smart, it's that you should work hard. It's just do, do, do, until you can't do anymore.' "

Much of this pressure came from existing corporate structures and culture. As I mentioned, one of the easiest measures available to evaluate someone's performance is hours on the job, so long hours are often recognized and rewarded. If the boss happens to stroll through the office at six o'clock and sees you sitting at your desk with a furrowed brow, typing furiously, it probably looks like you're a dedicated and committed employee. The empty desk beside you might belong to a coworker who apparently doesn't take the job as seriously.

We have internalized these values to the point where many of us are willing and devoted believers. We have converted to the religion of long hours and have faith that working without cease is not just the best way to get a promotion, but the best way to *live.* Everywhere you look you'll find advice on how to "hack" your habits in order to achieve better results. The internet is filled with articles and advice about how to use every possible waking moment in order to get ahead in your career.

An entrepreneur known as Gary Vee (short for Vaynerchuk) has reached the bestseller list four times by dispensing advice for making money and increasing one's influence. He tells fans: "Working nineteen hours a day every day for the last twenty years has been easy for me because it's the only gear I ever knew." Working at least twelve hours at a time is what Vaynerchuk calls "the straightest road to success."

He's wrong, of course. Study after study shows that long hours are counterproductive and have diminishing returns over time. But most of us feel, intuitively, that working more will help us get ahead. Time equals money, so more time will equal more money, right? "If you want bling-bling, if you want to buy the jets?" Vaynerchuk told an audience of fans. "Work. That's how you get it."

We eat that up. It *sounds* true, it seems to have worked for Gary Vee and Bill Gates, and that's why so many of us choose not to take our vacation time: We're afraid we'll lose ground. There are many workers who don't get paid vacation, but even those who do choose not to use it.

Jared Yates Sexton at Georgia Southern University told me about a conversation he overheard after a faculty meeting. He says, "One of my colleagues said of another, 'She takes a lot of vacations.' That was an insult. The implication was she was slacking because she doesn't work through the entire summer." It doesn't matter if the employee handbook tells people to work all summer or to relax on a beach somewhere. Policies that are not explicitly laid out in employee handbooks are often enforced through shaming.

This is a particularly American problem. The United States is the only nation in the OECD (Organisation for Economic Cooperation and Development) that doesn't require employers to give paid vacation time to staff. In the EU, workers are guaranteed a minimum of twenty days off with pay, and Europeans are generally good about taking it.

Here's the irony: Staying on the job may well be impeding your career advancement. It accomplishes the opposite of what's intended. Even though Americans say they're afraid to take time off because they may be punished, research shows that people who take at least eleven days of vacation are more likely to get a raise than people who take ten days or less.

I have found this to be true in my own life. The more I turn down invitations to speak and zealously guard my days off, the more invitations I receive and the higher the proffered fees. Since 2014, I have slashed my working hours, but my income has more than quadrupled. I'm not saying that the reduction in hours has led to more money, but working less has certainly not cost me any money or professional standing.

I was horrified recently to read a piece in the *Harvard Business Review* from a marketing strategist named Dorie Clark. Clark warns that taking time off often means falling behind, and she stresses the importance of using every waking moment to make connections. "It's easy and alluring to say to yourself,

Take more vacation: you deserve it!" Clark writes. "But a better question to ask is whether you're ready to leverage your vacation—to truly dedicate the time and effort needed to become the kind of person, and professional, that you want to be."

Please don't "leverage your vacation." In fact, if you spend your vacation time truly separated from work stress, research shows you're more likely to return to work refreshed and ultimately perform better on the job. "Leveraging your vacation" could cause you to make more mistakes and bad decisions while at work. It will probably backfire.

Decades of research disprove this theory that constant "hustle" helps you achieve. Repeated studies show that taking time off boosts productivity, creativity, and creative problem-solving. It can even strengthen your immune system, making it less likely that you'll get sick and be forced to stay home with a cold. So why don't Americans take a break? Because we've been brainwashed to believe that hard work, on its own, is the key to success.

In an op-ed that protests against the unhealthy work ethic of Silicon Valley, Daniel Heinemeier Hansson points out that Charles Darwin worked only four hours a day and Kobe Bryant put in only six hours a day during the off-season. Hansson, the founder of Basecamp and the bestselling author of *Rework*, says, "Don't tell me that there's something uniquely demanding about building yet another fucking startup that dwarfs the accomplishments of *The Origin of Species* or winning five championship rings. It's bullshit. Extractive, counterproductive bullshit peddled by people who either need a narrative to explain their personal sacrifices and regrets or who are in a position to treat the lives and well-being of others like cannon fodder."

Lest you think this is all hot air, Hansson has put his money where his philosophy is. Hansson's employees work forty hours a week for most of the year and only thirty-two hours during the summer months. In a 2017 op-ed, he wrote, "Workaholism is a disease. We need treatment and coping advice for those afflicted, not cheerleaders for their misery." If it is a disease, it's the worst kind: the kind we won't admit we have and therefore don't seek to treat. *Workaholic* should not be a compliment or a humblebrag—it should be a cry for help.

If you still believe, after all this, that you have to work more than forty hours a week, that it's not possible to get your work done while putting in less time, let me try a little harder to convince you otherwise. Perhaps you'll be swayed by the experience of one workplace that sought to discover what happened when they stepped off the excessive-hours treadmill.

In 2015, administrators at one of the largest hospitals in Europe, Sahlgrenska University Hospital, were concerned about burnout among staff and decided to cut work hours for the orthopedic unit. More than one hundred nurses and doctors started working six-hour days. I'm sure you can imagine how revolutionary that decision was in an industry famed for its punishing schedules, where cots are set up in breakrooms so that nurses and residents can snatch a catnap from time to time.

It's a good bet that administrators were nervous about the experiment, but since cutting down shifts, the orthopedic unit has become *more* productive and efficient, not less so. The executive director, Anders Hyltander, told the *New York Times* that sick days have been slashed to almost nothing. "For years, we've been told that an eight-hour day is optimal," Hyltander said. "But if you want to increase productivity, be open to new ideas."

The old idea is that long hours equal more work and better people. That's a very old idea indeed. While it was somewhat intentional on the part of corporate management to convince people that long hours make you a better person and more prone to success, part of this delusion has been an unintentional result of "improvements" in our working lives. For example, executives have repeatedly invested in comfy sofas and picnic tables and carefully landscaped atria in order to make workers feel more at home. The intention was mostly benevolent.

Workers spent a lot of time at the office, and management wanted to make the environment as beautiful and pleasant as possible. As a result, for many office workers, there is not much difference between the comfort levels of the office and the home. The office can "feel" like a second home to some, and managers make the mistake of saying "We are all family" in order to promote a feeling of camaraderie.

But the office is not your home and your coworkers are not your family. You can be laid off from work on any day, which is not generally true in a family, and I would hope your workplace doesn't force you to tolerate the dysfunction that's common in personal relationships. Creating a homey environment for our jobs has confused us, leading many to believe they can fulfill their need for social connection and belongingness through their employment, though that's not usually the case.

While it's important to create an environment that's safe, comfortable, and supportive of creative thinking, it's also crucial that there be a clear distinction between being on the clock and off. "Work has become more than work," the Columbia professor Silvia Bellezza told me. "Work now fulfills some of the needs for socialization that before only time with family and friends would satisfy." As our personal lives have become lonelier and more isolated, lots of people would rather stay at work, where they at least have some social contact.

Another misguided effort was the creation of open office plans. In this case, the motive was noble and positive: Executives sought to create more cohesive teams and to encourage social interaction. In the end, the effect has been the exactly the opposite. Years of research show open office plans actually make people *less* likely to talk to each other. Having no possibility of privacy causes stress and therefore discourages creative thought. We put people on display and they retreated. Can you blame them? And many experts predicted that open offices would lead to a bump in productivity, but once more the results were often the opposite. Some managers believed they could induce employees to focus on their work by making it difficult to conceal what they were doing. But Ethan Bernstein, professor of organizational behavior at Harvard, discovered that when the walls came down, employees put *more* effort into concealing their activities. They found new reasons to leave the office or linger in the breakroom; some even created secret codes to communicate with coworkers without being overheard. Workers began using conference rooms so they could shut the door or they started coming in early so they could work alone. Bernstein suggested that "creating zones of privacy may, under certain conditions, increase performance."

I understand it's usually hard to foresee the negative impacts of our choices, especially when the intention is to make someone else's life better. Here again, let's consider a striking difference between Europe and the United States. For a long time, stores in Europe didn't open on the weekends. Until very recently, there was a Sunday shopping ban in countries like Germany, Denmark, Hungary, Spain, and the United Kingdom. Such a ban still exists in Poland.

Many of us might see such policies as inconvenient. Certainly, it's more expedient to be able to buy clothes and tools any day of the week. But Silvia Bellezza says Americans have paid a price for the convenience of weekend shopping. "People in Europe need to run errands during the week," she told me. "So, they leave work on time. In the U.S., you can get your shopping done at any time. Some stores are open twenty-four hours a day." That means people are willing to remain in the office, knowing it won't affect their ability to get things done at home.

Perhaps the most disastrous unintended consequence of a positive intention dates all the way back to Henry Ford in the early twentieth century. On May 1, 1926, Ford Motor Company became one of the first to institute a forty-hour week for its employees. Ford had already created the five-dollar workday in 1914, a decision that had profound impacts on labor everywhere and helped create a new class of consumers: employees with enough disposable income to afford the very vehicles they helped build. Ford is often credited with helping to create the middle class in the United States.

While the decision to limit working hours to no more than forty was important for work-life balance, Ford told reporters he was motivated more by capitalism than philanthropy. "Leisure," Ford told the magazine *World's Work,* "is an indispensable ingredient in a growing consumer market, because working people need to have enough free time to find uses for consumer products, including automobiles."

In other words, Ford increased worker pay so that employees could buy his products, and he limited their work hours so they'd have time to shop. Many, many corporations have followed Ford's lead. Being a loyal customer became a mark of a good worker at most companies, and eventually politicians picked up this rallying cry, encouraging citizens to shop in order to demonstrate love for their nation. Two weeks after the September 11 attacks, for example, President George W. Bush told citizens, "Do your business around the country. . . . Get down to Disney World in Florida. Take your families and enjoy life."

The idea that spending is good for a nation's health is a very recent one. Not all that long ago, overspending was considered immoral and indebtedness was seen as a character flaw. In the 1800s, many European governments created savings banks at local post offices and even at some schools, to encourage young people to put money aside.

"All this fostered cultures of saving that endure today in many advanced economies," writes Sheldon Garon, author of *Beyond Our Means: Why America Spends While the World Saves.* I need not remind you that the 1800s were the heyday of the Industrial Revolution, so this switch from saving to spending is just one more change that has come about since we became mechanized.

The household savings rate in the European Union hovers at about 10 percent. That's close to what it was in 1960 in the

United States. Now it's fallen to about 2 percent for Americans, and the American approach to spending may be spreading. In 2017, for the first time in three decades, British citizens spent more than they made. Australia has seen a similar change: Savings fell from nearly 10 percent in 1959 to just over 2 percent in 2018.

In many nations, citizens are encouraged to shop more in order to keep corporate profits high. Here's how it works: Productivity increased in the twentieth century but working hours have remained the same. Instead of making 100 video game consoles in forty hours of work, we're now making 150. Those extra fifty consoles need to go somewhere. Corporations clearly don't want to pay to store that merchandise in a warehouse and they don't give their workers time off while the excess is sold.

So consumers are told to keep businesses strong by purchasing more things. "The biggest gift that the United States could get during the holiday season," writes Larry Light of CBS's MoneyWatch, "is robust shopping by the American consumer, who is now the primary engine powering economic performance." An officer from a local machinists' union in Florida wrote an op-ed in 2011 that declared, "The answer to America's economic problems is in our own backyard. The answer is: buy American."

In recent years, younger people have resisted that pressure and have consequently been shamed by the broader society. Millennials are choosing to spend their money on experiences instead of things. Rather than choosing jobs that offer the highest pay, younger people are looking for employers who share their values, and 84 percent believe they are duty-bound to change the world. Not surprisingly, the global economy blames millennials for killing off the diamond market, department stores, the auto industry, the travel industry, and casinos.

Remember that collectively, we chose to take the benefits of productivity and invest them into more product instead of shorter working hours. Therefore, as supply increased, the cost of many things that were once considered luxury items fell rapidly. Beginning in the 1980s and '90s, even middle-class families were able to afford multiple TV sets. The first cell phone, a Motorola DynaTAC, cost about $4,000 in 1983. A first-generation iPhone cost $600 twenty years later. A microwave set you back almost $600 in the early eighties. I walked through my local Target today and found a large microwave on sale for less than forty bucks.

While all of these forces were pulling and tugging on national economies, a fascinating cultural evolution occurred in the late twentieth century. Leaving out the extreme ends of the income spectrum (billionaires and their millionaire friends, along with the poor on the other end), the cultural emphasis shifted from luxury to busyness. People stopped bragging about their flat-screen TVs and started "complaining" about their packed schedules. Status was awarded not because you had an iPhone; everyone seemed to have an iPhone. Instead, people earned respect according to how little free time they had.

When I was on my train ride around the country, one young woman who was traveling from Boston to New York asked if I'd been laid off. "I just can't imagine how you have the time. If I took two weeks off, my department would fall apart. Literally fall apart," she told me. Obviously, I don't think her colleagues would be incapable of functioning without her presence, but her message to me was clear: I am indispensable. I am busy because I am important.

This is not just anecdotal evidence collected from one woman on one day riding one train. Complaining about how little time we have has become one of the most common activities of the late 1990s and early 2000s. Researchers noted the change years ago and began investigating the phenomenon of busyness as status symbol.

In 1899, the economist and sociologist Thorstein Veblen published his hugely influential book *The Theory of the Leisure Class*. In it, he remarked that one of the most powerful indicators of personal success was "conspicuous abstention from labor." Veblen might be very surprised to see that over the ensuing one hundred years, idleness came to mean not success but poverty.

This is a particular problem in the United States, Canada, Australia, and Britain. Studies have shown that people assume someone wearing a Bluetooth headset (who presumably needs to multitask and take calls all day) is of higher status than someone wearing headphones, who may be listening to music and simply enjoying themselves. Again and again in research studies, when presented with a choice between two similar individuals, we say that the busier person is the more important person.

Essentially, bragging about how busy you are gives the impression that you are valuable and in high demand, like my young train friend. Instead of wearing expensive products and demonstrating that one's clothing has high value, a person who's very busy is implicitly bragging about their intrinsic worth, their own intelligence. They might talk about all the appointments and tasks on their calendar or they may respond to most invitations by saying, "I'll have to check my schedule." When you ask how they are, instead of saying, "Fine," they might say, "Busy!"

One of the reasons chronic busyness is so common in places like the United States and not in places like Italy, is that Americans have long valued *earned* status, which is a side effect of the myth of the self-made man. Not your family name or net worth but your cramped schedule shows your inherent value. What's more, having no free time is an indication of how hard you're working, and hard work garners nearly immediate respect.

That's not to say that expensive goods are no longer sought after or used to signify status. Back in 1899, when Veblen was writing about "conspicuous consumption," he talked about the widespread hunger to buy ever more unnecessary but costly items. "Leisure held the first place at the start, and came to hold a rank very much above wasteful consumption of goods," Veblen wrote. "From that point onward, consumption has gained ground, until, at present, it unquestionably holds the primacy." That is all still true for the very highest earners who seek to buy ever-larger houses, helicopters, and boats, but it's not generally true for the rest of us.

Conspicuous consumption reached its peak during the waning days of the twentieth century. In 1970, the Swedish economist Staffan Linder wrote about the "harried leisure class." He described them as "harried" because the explosion in the number of available items and their relative affordability —one could always find *something* to buy, regardless of income level—caused a unique kind of stress.

Remember, during the 1980s and '90s, the cost of items once considered far beyond the reach of the middle class was rapidly dropping. Productivity was increasing steadily, manufacturers were creating warehouses full of goods, and prices kept falling in order to keep the products moving off the shelves.

Economists began to realize that John Maynard Keynes may have been wrong when he posited that people work only to buy what they *need*. Instead, people may continue buying in order to experience, again and again, that flush of pleasure that accompanies the acquisition of something new. We get a shot of dopamine in our brains when we purchase something, and we can become literally addicted to acquisition.

In the book *Revisiting Keynes,* Lorenzo Pecchi and Gustavo Piga argue that our excitement over buying a new thing is intense but short-lived. "The average consumer," they said, "grows accustomed to what he has purchased and . . . rapidly aspires to own the next product in line." So while Keynes predicted that we'd all be working very little by now, the rise in unnecessary consumption was part of what made him wrong.

The glorification of consumerism creates a vicious cycle. We work longer and longer hours in order to buy products that we think will make our lives better, we stop enjoying them fairly quickly, the products themselves require time and maintenance that cut into our free time, this makes us unhappy, so we decide to relieve our feelings of sadness with a new product. Rinse and repeat.

You might think this problem would disappear in the higher-income brackets because the wealthy often have enough money to buy whatever they want and don't feel a need to make more money in order to purchase more things. Are you getting used to hearing that as it turns out, the opposite is true?

Recall the 1965 quote I shared earlier from economist and sociologist Gary S. Becker: "When people are paid more, they work longer hours because work is so much more profitable than leisure." This remains true for even the top earners.

To my dismay, I found myself caught in this trap. I would set aside a week for relaxation, then an offer would come in that was too good to turn down. *I can't say no to that amount of money,* I would think. If someone offered me $200 to fly to Denver and give a speech, I'd have no trouble saying no. As the amount goes higher, though, the money begins to seem more valuable than the time off *even though I don't need the extra money.* And I'm not even in the upper-income tiers, where I'd be willing to bet the offers are even harder to refuse.

Since there is always something else to buy, there is never enough money for those of us in the middle class, and that means we are never working enough hours. The end result is that our off-hours start to feel stressful. Time is money, and we feel guilty when we waste it doing unproductive and unprofitable things.

We can see the shift in what's considered high status when we examine the data on who works the most. In the 1980s, blue-collar workers worked longer hours than did salaried employees, meaning that a lower income meant longer workdays. That has since been turned on its head. Now college-educated workers are twice as likely as their blue-collar counterparts to work more than forty hours a week.

In the years between 1985 and 2005, people without a high school diploma gained about eight hours of leisure time per week. So today, generally speaking, the less you make, the more free time you have. It's not too much of a stretch to assume that the more hours you work, the more likely people are to see you as important and wealthy.

It's not cool to have time to spare time now. "When I was a kid," Graeme Maxton told me, "my father was in the golf club. You had to wait ten years to get in. Today, you can get in instantly because people are spending their time working and shopping. Hobbies have disappeared for much the same reason. People don't have time to golf anymore."

A survey of golfers in 2015 showed most think it takes too long to play eighteen holes. Players younger than forty-five said they'd prefer to play for only ninety minutes or so, and many courses now offer nine-hole games. This impatience shows up in all kinds of industries: People even listen to podcasts and audiobooks at double or even triple speed in order to get through them more quickly.

Here's the biggest irony of all this: We skimp on our personal lives in order to have more time for our careers, but we don't get the return on our investment that we expect. *Overwork* is defined as more than fifty hours per week, and people who put in those kinds of hours make only 6 percent more than those with more reasonable schedules. So if you make an average wage of $45,000 a year, you'll get an extra $2,500 in exchange for working excessive hours.

Deep down, I think we understand where our priorities should lie. When people are asked in surveys, they usually say they'd rather have time off than more money. Polls in Europe and North America repeatedly show people putting a higher value on leisure time than on stuff. In response, corporations have invested very heavily in changing our minds on that subject. As the writer J. R. Benjamin said, "One reason over a trillion dollars a year is spent on marketing in the USA is to try to undermine our natural tendency to want free, liberated time."

There are effective ways to counteract all that brainwashing. One solution is to take up a hobby that requires a lot of time. I've started doing cross-stitch again, even though one of my friends warned that I could never sell my finished work because people aren't willing to pay for all the hours it takes to make. I don't care. I'll continue making my beautiful embroidery that takes ungodly hours, and adamantly refuse to put a price on it. It makes me happy. Every time I look at the careful stitches and brilliant colors, I feel proud of what I accomplished. That feeling is priceless. Who knows? Maybe I'll start making story tapes again too.

We have sacrificed quite a bit at the altar of hard work and long hours. We have traded our privacy, our communities, our hobbies, and our peace of mind for habits that are more commercially profitable. The overriding question is this: Is it worth it? For the past few decades, our answer has been yes, but it may be time to think again.

Chapter 5

WORK COMES HOME

> The quest for achieving peak productivity is now akin to a religion, one consisting of high priests (time management gurus, life hack specialists, productivity coaches, headlining management professionals), various teachings (apps, tools, approaches, methods, reminders, workstation re-designs, forms of discipline), and millions of willing aspirants (early adopters, workshop participants, testifiers, devotees). A search for "how to be more productive" yields, at present count, 40,900,000 results.
>
> —ANDREW TAGGART

DO YOU REMEMBER THE push to set aside "quality time" with your kids back in the 1990s? I was just out of high school at that time and remember seeing that phrase splashed all over women's magazines at the grocery store, and hearing it discussed on talk shows. One of my college professors shortened it to "QT" and would say things like "My office hours end at three today. I'm due for a couple hours of QT with my kids."

This whole thing was a relatively short-lived fad. In 1997, *Newsweek* published a cover story called "The Myth of Quality Time." I became a parent about a year after that article appeared, when quality time had mostly fallen out of vogue. It was a ludicrous idea for me anyway. My fiancé was overseas with the military in Bosnia when my son was born. I was a single parent. Out of necessity, my son came with me everywhere, even to the office when he grew to be a toddler. There was no difference, for me, between quality time and normal time. When I had a moment to read with him or play a board game, I seized the opportunity.

Even though people rarely talk about quality time these days, the concept behind it survives. The idea that you can design an hour with your kids that's so excellent and impactful that it makes up for frequently staying late at work is an unspoken principle in many homes. That idea started in the workplace, where managers have long believed that they can create an environment that increases the quality of work.

Back in the early nineties, when families were still enthusiastic about the idea of quality time, the sociologist Arlie Russell Hochschild was spending her summers observing the work and home lives of the employees at a large American corporation. Many of them talked to her about quality time, and Hochschild said the intent was to transfer "the cult of efficiency from office to home. Instead of nine hours a day with a child, we declare ourselves capable of getting the 'same result' with one more intensely focused total quality hour. . . . Our family bonds are being recalibrated to achieve greater productivity in less time."

I totally understand the guilt a parent feels when they repeatedly say, "Go play in your room. I need to get this done." I know how crushing it can be to finally walk in the door in the evening, anxious to see your kid, only to find that he's already in bed. It's no surprise that we would try to solve these problems at home by using the same techniques that seem to work so well in the office.

In truth, we have brought home much more than just the idea of quality time. Most of us have worked hard to make our homes as efficient as possible, and that has caused problems of its own.

We bring more and more of our work with us when we leave the office, structure our off-hours around the computer and the smartphone, and design our lives to better accommodate our jobs. Perhaps to make us feel better about it, we bring a little of home into the office. We celebrate birthdays at the workplace and bring our kids to work (as I did), work out in office gyms, shop for holiday presents from office computers.

This is not all bad news, of course. The blurring of lines between work and home isn't necessarily a bad thing. There are advantages to this strategy. Perhaps writing a report at home means you can spend a couple extra hours with your loved ones. Maybe the colorful paintings and lush green plants at the office help relax you and spur creativity. Perhaps you're fighting with your partner and the office feels like a refuge from the hostility at home.

In the final accounting, though, it's not an even trade. We know a lot about how people from all over the world view their jobs, and so we know that much of the traffic between work and home has been one-way. In other words, in the battle between the office and the living room, the office has mostly won.

When it comes to life philosophies and personal habits, the past few decades have seen us internalize what we've learned on the job and apply it to our daily lives and intimate relationships. You can find telltale signs of the office in our kitchens, our living rooms, even our beds.

I wouldn't want us to bring our personal habits into the office, of course. I don't want my employees to keep their workspace as cluttered as their kitchens, and I definitely don't want them calling me to chat about their cousins and BFFs. That would be very inappropriate. But it's also inappropriate to run your personal life as though you're adhering to an employee handbook.

While CEOs and executives structured their businesses around the concept of constant growth, we began to do the same with our lives. We now believe it's possible and even laudable to be constantly improving and tweaking and changing. Not in the long term, mind you, but on a daily basis. We make checklists for our eating and our exercise and our meditation. We create digital reminders to write in our journals or read a book.

We're not generally interested in growth that happens over time, either. Instead, we search for shortcuts, buying books that promise we'll master Spanish in five hours. I was strolling through a bookstore recently and saw an entire rack of books dedicated to learning at lightning speed: *30-Second Psychology, 30-Second Economics, 30-Second Genetics.*

I want to be clear, from the start, that I think it's good to look for opportunities to improve yourself. That's a wonderful impulse. But, as with technology, the problem is not in the tool but in its overuse. Improvement is healthy, but not every moment of your day should be leveraged in an attempt to make you a better person. If you're searching for the fastest way to learn guitar because you also have to squeeze in yoga and keto cooking recipes and homemade charcoal facial peels, you have left no time to simply be the person you are. You are leaving no space for rest and contentment.

In 2016, the self-help industry was worth nearly $10 billion in the United States alone. By 2022, it's expected to be worth more than $13 billion. Many people believe their lives, minds, and bodies can be hacked, tinkered with, and improved in a never-ending search for peak productivity.

Why just make a cake when you can search through Pinterest and find the *best* cake recipe with the cutest decoration ideas? Almost no one searches for a "good workout routine," instead looking for the "ultimate workout." We want the fastest, most efficient method for reaching our goals, hopefully guaranteed by as many five-star reviews as possible.

"What I see is that we've taken the bourgeois virtue of hard work, or productivity," writes the consultant and trainer Andrew Taggart, "and applied it to ourselves with ruthless persistence." The word *ruthless* is well chosen here, since I see people exhausting themselves in this pursuit of constant improvement and the most efficient life possible, often based not on what they really want but on a list they read of the things successful people do every day.

Schedules, apps, eating plans, expensive devices . . . anything that we believe will save us a little time and make us a little better. One of my friends keeps four journals: one for running, one for eating, one for daily tasks, and yet another for gratitude. Individually, the intent of those journals is good; taken together, it's simply too much.

Oftentimes, all these little tweaks and hacks aren't even more efficient. Consider the challenge of taking notes, for example. If you've attended a college course recently, you probably saw a teacher facing a room full of open laptops. Most students take notes with their computers, and many working people do the same. We bring our laptops into meetings and continue typing while listening to a conference call.

If your goal is rote dictation, then typing into a laptop is definitely more efficient. Many students type so quickly that they can record nearly every word a professor utters. But we've known for years that using electronics to take notes is not the best way to understand what you're hearing or retain the information.

Let's put aside the possibility for distraction and the temptation, when using a laptop or tablet, to quickly check your email or surf the internet. A study out of Princeton and UCLA also found that even when the computer is used only to take notes, it's still inferior to writing in longhand when it comes to comprehension and retention. The report was titled "The Pen Is Mightier Than the Keyboard." Students who used their laptops did poorly when asked conceptual questions, despite recording more of what was said. When students write in longhand, they process the information they hear and record it in their own words. Those who use a laptop might be able to transcribe a lecture verbatim, but they simply don't learn as much.

Professor Susan Dynarski of the University of Michigan wrote an op-ed in the *New York Times* in 2017 explaining why she bans all electronics from her classrooms. She admits this policy may seem extreme but says, "The research is unequivocal: Laptops distract from learning, both for users and for those around them. It's not much of a leap to expect that electronics also undermine learning in high school classrooms or that they hurt productivity in meetings in all kinds of workplaces."

This, essentially, is the danger of making efficiency a goal in and of itself. We can become so focused on doing things more quickly that we lose sight of what's actually being accomplished. If you're getting down every word a professor says but understanding very little of the lecture, you'll have a tough time passing the class. So what is the real goal? Quickness and efficiency, or thoroughness and deep understanding?

I always take notes in longhand now, but since I love trees, I don't use paper. I found a tablet on which I write in cursive, and then it converts my longhand notes into text in a Word document. I never get a full transcription of what I've heard, just the gist, but the act of having to decide what to write down helps me remember the material.

I make decisions constantly about what's important and what's really being said. Therefore, my notes are more personal and more helpful, in the long run, than the more complete notes I would take with my tablet. Less productive, since I'm literally writing fewer words, but more useful.

"We adopt the illusion," Andrew Taggart says, "that personal productivity *is itself* the end of suffering, or *is itself* happiness, when in actuality, the aim of personal productivity is to enable the work-society to continue. . . . The truth is that we are its tools." In other words, we use laptops because we think recording 80 percent of what's said is inherently better than getting only 50 percent. We strive to achieve peak productivity but forget that it's taking us further from our ultimate goal—learning.

I don't believe that if left to our own devices, we would naturally seek to work long hours and search for peak efficiency in everything we do, including doing laundry and playing games and reading novels. There is a wealth of historical data that suggests we prefer a balance of leisure and toil. But we have been convinced through more than two hundred years of propaganda that inactivity is the same as laziness, and that leisure is a shameful waste of time.

If you think I'm using the word *propaganda* metaphorically, you're wrong. Let's dial it back to the 1920s for a moment. The battle over work hours was still being fiercely fought throughout the industrialized world, but the workers were winning. The punishing days of the nineteenth century were far behind us, and workdays were getting shorter and shorter in most industries.

There seems to have been a realization among employers that they couldn't win a direct fight, so they used more subtle tactics learned during World War I. Employers realized they could borrow strategies from the War Department in order to motivate the production line.

A young Austrian immigrant had spent the war working for the Committee on Public Information (CPI), engaging in what he called "psychological warfare." The Cornell graduate was tasked with building public support for the war in the United States and overseas, and he was very good at it.

Edward Bernays would later say he learned an invaluable lesson while at the CPI office: The tactics he'd used during war "could be applied with equal facility to peacetime pursuits. In other words, what could be done for a nation at war could be done for organizations and people in a nation at peace." This slight man with his dark, sunken eyes, high forehead, and generous mustache is probably not familiar to most people today, but he changed our lives irrevocably.

Bernays is now known as the "Father of Spin." He helped make it fashionable for women to smoke in the late twenties by rebranding cigarettes as "Torches of Freedom" and symbols of feminist strength. His 1928 book, *Propaganda,* was hugely influential and put into practice by many men in power. "Those who manipulate this unseen mechanism of society constitute an invisible government which is the true ruling power of our country," Bernays wrote. "In almost every act of our daily lives, whether in the sphere of politics or business, in our social conduct or our ethical thinking, we are dominated by the relatively small number of persons . . . who understand the mental processes and social patterns of the masses."

Workers were manipulated to feel shame for even wanting to take time off. Company names became almost synonymous with *country.* Europe may have family crests, but America has company logos. In the 1920s, employers began putting up posters that scolded those who invested less than full effort while on the job. "Waste, carelessness, mistakes, loafing," one poster read. "Help us stop them before they stop us."

Another showed a soldier receiving a commendation in front of an unfurled American flag and read: "The efficient worker is always honored. His merit is recognized by all. Stand out from the crowd!" Yet another features an enormous clock backed by a skyline of smokestacks. "When the Call Comes, Answer Present," it urges. "When you are 'Off' someone else gets on to your opportunity! A day off may lose you much." These were daily affirmations created by employers, drilling in to workers' minds the principles that most benefited the company.

Employers also discovered they could pit their workers against one another to vie for promotions and raises, thereby encouraging people to stay longer than their coworkers and put in more hours than their "competition."

Somehow the same characteristics used to describe a good employee came to also describe a good husband or sister or friend: reliable, stable, hardworking, independent. The writer Maria Popova told the BBC: "The most pernicious thing [is] this tendency we have to apply productivity to realms of life that should, by their very nature, be devoid of that criterion."

Popova reports that she used to enjoy taking a camera with her everywhere and taking photos of what she saw. Now that she feels pressured to leverage her photos on social media, the camera "has become its own burden." I understand her dilemma. I love to walk but sometimes when the sole purpose of my jaunt is to meet my step goal, I dread leaving the house. What was a joy sometimes feels like drudgery because I've turned a pleasure into work.

Again, it should go without saying that it is natural to want to improve. We are biologically programmed to quickly become impatient with the status quo and to push for better things. But we've pushed it too far. What's more, we've lost sight of the fact that productivity is a *means* to an end, not a goal in and of itself. One time-use expert told Juliet Schor, "We have become walking résumés. If you're not doing something, you're not creating and defining who you are."

This compulsion to approach our lives in the same way we approach a project in the office is what helped make busyness a status symbol. In 2007, Tim Ferriss wrote *The 4-Hour Workweek*, which is full of instructions on how to cut down your work hours. I would enthusiastically support that idea, except that his goal is not to increase your free time but to leverage it.

In a blog post about his daily schedule, he says, "The goal was never to be idle." In his "off time," Ferriss does interviews and writes articles and trains in hiking or archery or martial arts. Everything he does is seemingly intended to help him reach ever-increasing goals with ruthless efficiency. He posted a rundown of a typical day, and his schedule includes eating, working out, writing, taking an ice bath, and then relaxing after eleven p.m. Ferriss says he does his "best writing" between one and four a.m.

Ferriss is just one of many people who hope to suck the marrow out of every moment of their day, to never waste time that could be spent moving toward a new achievement. A shortened workweek is something I endorse; torturing every minute in order to make every moment productive is not.

I've mentioned that social status became dependent, in the late twentieth century, less on wealth and more on busyness. That trend began in the 1990s and has only intensified since. Social media has fed this obsession with performative busyness. I say "performative" because sometimes the purpose of an activity seems to be solely to take pictures and post them or write about the experience in a blog post.

As a result, people are more likely to attend events and engage in activities that will look good on their Instagram feed. I was recently in a national park and stopped to admire a little clearing in the trees, lazily crossed by a slow-moving brook. There were two squirrels playing chase around an ash tree, and wild indigo swayed in the breeze. The scene was so beautiful that it felt unreal.

My first instinct was to take a picture, but I chose not to because I wanted that moment to be more precious than an Instagram post. I had come to the park to enjoy the sunshine and the landscape. I wanted to escape from work, not turn my hike into an extension of my professional branding.

That anecdote makes me sound relaxed about all this, but that's misleading. For most of my adult life, I have thought that if I'm not making pesto from scratch, I could at least do some yoga, and if not yoga, I could at least write a quick blog post. In many ways, I make decisions based on how the choices and outcomes might affect my résumé of life.

For many of us, this drive to leverage every moment eventually gave rise to an obsession with life hacking and a pursuit of ever more complex, arcane, and counterintuitive methods to accomplish what we probably know how to do already. Not only should we fill our off-hours with photo-worthy pursuits, but those pursuits should be awe-inspiring. If we can't get our friends to "like" our hobbies, then what's the point?

John Pavlus wrote a piece in 2012 called "Confessions of a Recovering Lifehacker." Pavlus had a crisis of the soul upon discovering how much time he spent reading articles about tweaking every aspect of his personal and professional life. "Maybe all the time I spend looking for better ways to do things is keeping me from, well, *doing things*. It's like running on a treadmill: you might get in really good shape, I guess, but you never actually go anywhere."

Pavlus asks if life hacking is, in truth, a way to focus on small, measurable tasks instead of asking ourselves big, hard questions about what we do with our time and what our larger priorities are. A woman I know frantically shakes her arm every hour while working on the computer, so she can fool her Fitbit into thinking she's taken 250 steps. I guess she's hacking her exercise, but it's not making her healthier.

Isn't good health the goal of wearing a Fitbit, not getting a certain number of steps? I ask myself that whenever I find myself walking in circles around my kitchen, staring at my watch so I can stop as soon as I reach a certain number of steps.

In many ways, I think we've lost sight of the purpose of free time. We seem to immediately equate idleness with laziness, but those two things are very different. *Leisure* is not a synonym for *inactive*. Idleness offers an opportunity for play, something people rarely indulge in these days. I mentioned that golf courses are offering new methods to make the game go faster, but there are actually many sports we no longer have time for. ESPN published an article in 2014 with the headline "Playground Basketball Is Dying." "The courts are empty," the piece says. "The nets dangling by a thread. The crowds that used to stand four-deep are gone, and so are the players." The movie *The Sandlot* will soon be an anachronism, since the number of kids playing baseball has fallen by millions.

Sports are just one example of this phenomenon. Recent surveys have shown that membership has declined in PTAs, unions, churches, environmental groups, and political parties. Nearly half of people say they don't like joining any groups at all, and more than half say they don't have time, even if they wanted to.

The point is, we engage in busyness that is mostly goal-oriented and designed to create a public persona, rather than hobbies that are *merely* intended to enrich our lives. Even parenting is often centered on amassing achievements and résumé-fillers. The social psychologist Harry Triandis points out that when a culture is focused on individuals and not on communities, people tend to emphasize achievement over affiliation. And the sociology professor Philip Cohen told the *Economist*, "Parents are now afraid of doing less than their neighbors. It can feel like an arms race."

Child-rearing often requires a slower pace because children can't always be forced to do what they're told at the pace we prefer. I remember hurrying my son along through a store, telling him to stop staring at the toys and "pick up the pace." In protest, he threw himself down in the aisle and started crying.

Speed and efficiency are, by their nature, antithetical to introspection and intimacy. The kind of social consciousness required to get to know another person intimately and to understand the emotional landscape of a community requires time and focus, two things most people don't think they have.

But time and focus are essential in our relationships. Scientists have found that in order to understand and empathize with other people, you must be capable of introspection. And as a 2009 report points out, the "type of introspective thought process necessary for understanding culturally shaped social knowledge is slower and requires additional time compared with the rapid multitasking, and parallel processing" of smartphones and laptops. We are looking for faster and faster ways to reach our goals, and so the skills that require time and patience—the social skills—are eroding.

Another by-product of the "time is money" mind-set has been the dramatic increase in distraction. Psychologists say modern society often suffers from a split consciousness or "absent presence," in which we are never fully paying attention to what we're doing or saying. This also has its roots in the nineteenth century, because that's when populations began to move from rural areas into cities.

People living in villages and on farms generally interacted with a limited number of people. They only kept track of one to two hundred people, so remembering birthdays and personal quirks was fairly simple. When people migrated into cities en masse, that number of interactions exploded, and people began to experience what's called "urban overload."

The sociologist Georg Simmel spoke in 1903 about our tendency to conserve our "psychic energy" by filtering out what we see and hear, keeping our human interactions as superficial as possible. Not only was it impossible to remember personal details about all the people we encountered on the city streets, but it was psychologically draining to try.

The sense that we are overwhelmed and must protect ourselves from intimacy has been exacerbated by technology. Computers and smartphones added information overload to the mix, and a constant pressure to respond to others followed. That intensified the conviction among many of us that chatting with others was just too much to handle.

Our attention is now nearly always divided, because we seem to be always working on something. Our hobbies have become goals. Our homes have become offices and our free time is not free. These are some of the changes that have occurred over the past two hundred years. That doesn't necessarily mean all of the changes have been bad or harmful. The question we must answer is: Where is the line? How are we helping ourselves, and how are we hurting?

Chapter 6

THE BUSIEST GENDER

> Lay down at five, jump up at six, and start all over again
> 'Cause I'm a woman! W-O-M-A-N, I'll say it again.
>
> —"I'M A WOMAN,"
> *Lyrics by Jerome Lieber*

I RECENTLY GAVE A speech at the Massachusetts Conference for Women, and the speaker who preceded me explained that women must be deliberate when negotiating with male colleagues because men aren't as skilled at multitasking as women are. In my head, I thought, *Women can't multitask, either. That's a delusion.*

It's a delusion many people share, and there are hints of truth in it. I used to put multitasking on my résumé under "Special Skills." It wasn't until I read the actual research proving that the human mind can't truly do two things at once that I started to doubt my own abilities. Some animal brains can multitask, like the pigeon's, but the human mind falls short of the pigeon's on this one very specific skill. What we do is not work on two things at once but rapidly switch from one task to another. That's our form of "multitasking."

I have talked about multitasking before in connection with conversation, as the attempt to both talk with a friend and check your email inevitably leads to distraction and reduced intimacy. But the main reason we try to multitask is because we believe it's more efficient and ultimately increases our productivity. As our obsession with hyperproductivity has increased, so has our belief that we are able to multitask and that it helps us get more done in less time.

The truth is wholly the opposite in almost every circumstance, if neuroscience is to be believed. In study after study, we've found that we are slower at completing tasks when we switch from one activity to another than we are when we simply repeat the same activity. In other words, if you shut down every tab of your browser, mute your phone, and close your email inbox, you'll finish the memo you're writing in significantly less time.

Switching back and forth is not efficient. The more complex the task we are switching to, the longer it takes our brain to adjust. The accumulated cost can be so high that the American Psychological Association recommends that we "choose strategies that boost [our brain's] efficiency—above all, by avoiding multitasking, especially with complex tasks."

For people like me who spent years doing not two things but three or four things at once, the news is even worse. Research shows that people who think of themselves as "heavy multitaskers" are worse at distinguishing between useful information and irrelevant details. We also tend to be less organized mentally (it's chaos up there) and have *more* trouble switching from one task to another, not less. Practice at multitasking makes us less perfect.

And here's the worst news of all: "Heavy multitaskers" have the same trouble sorting through information and organizing their thoughts *even when they aren't multitasking.* This suggests that repeated attempts to make your mind do something it's not designed to do can actually do damage to your gray matter. The psychologist Clifford Nass of Stanford told NPR that people who multitask often "are worse at most kinds of thinking not only required for multitasking but what we generally think of as involving deep thought." Over time, Nass said, "their cognitive processes were impaired."

Here's a wrinkle, though: Women may actually be better at multitasking than men. This is the kind of nuance that I love about science: Women aren't *good* at it; they're just generally better than men. An interesting experiment conducted in Switzerland suggests that estrogen may help women's brains better handle the rapid switching from one task to another.

Keep in mind that we're not talking about complex activities. The researchers asked participants to walk on a treadmill while identifying the color in which some words were printed. Women under the age of sixty performed better than men and older women. When the older women and men were asked to concentrate on the assigned task, the coordination of their swinging arms, something we rarely think about consciously, decreased. The right arm slowed dramatically, and it's important to note that the swing of the right arm is controlled by the same side of the brain involved in sorting words and colors: the prefrontal cortex. Researchers noted that estrogen receptors are probably also located in that part of the brain, and so the presence or absence of estrogen could explain the difference in performance between men and postmenopausal women.

Those results are not conclusive, of course, but they are suggestive. And we can add that study to other research into gender differences, including an experiment carried out in Russia. Scientists put 140 people through a number of relatively simple cognitive tests, all related to switching tasks and focus, and they discovered that women had to put in less mental effort in order to multitask. Svetlana Kuptsova, one author of the study, said the results "suggest that women might find it easier than men to switch attention and their brains do not need to mobilize extra resources in doing so, as opposed to male brains."

So when it comes to simple tasks (note: writing emails and talking on the phone or checking your social media are not simple tasks), women might be better at switching back and forth than men. It's also true that neuroscientists don't condemn as harshly the practice of trying to do two uncomplicated things at the same time, like talking on the phone while folding laundry. But, and this is a big but, when it comes to more complex tasks, including most of the things we do while on the job, there's no evidence that women are better at multitasking, and there's plenty of evidence that trying to do it is really terrible for your brain.

The issue of multitasking is gendered because women, in my experience, are more likely to think they're good at multitasking and much more likely to spend their days trying to do too many things at the same time. So let me add yet one more data point to this discussion: Women are probably more damaged by the belief that multitasking is not only possible but good for productivity.

The sociologist Barbara Schneider and her colleagues wanted to figure out if multitasking was stressful for most people. She discovered that men were more likely to think multitasking was pleasurable but were also less likely to engage in it. Women reported multitasking for nearly fifty hours a week and it stressed them out. The group that was most stressed by trying to do multiple things at the same time was mothers.

Men said they felt relieved when they headed home from work, but women felt the opposite. Some women even referred to the hours just after work as "arsenic time." "Because the first thing that they had to start worrying about was getting dinner, interfacing with their kids, dealing with all of the household chores that needed to be done," Schneider told NPR. The research clearly shows stress rises as women walk through their doors, knowing they must not only continue to respond to work emails but also handle personal administrative duties in the place that is supposed to be a haven. They may be mentally running through a list of tasks that need to be accomplished before they can really relax.

Even when they're at work, women tend to put more pressure on themselves. Data collected by the Captivate Network shows men are 35 percent more likely to take a break while on the job, "just to relax." Men are also more likely to go out to lunch, take a walk, and take personal time during working hours. Melanie Shreffler, director of the Cassandra Report, told *Forbes,* "These women worked like crazy in school, and in college, and then they get into the workforce and they are exhausted."

So if there is a gender difference, it may be less about biology and more about women's reluctance to relax, combined with societal pressures to do more work around both the home and the workplace.

Although women have been working for millennia, they first began to flood into the workplace in the 1970s. That era is often referred to as the "Quiet Revolution," and the revolution is still going on nearly a half-century later. Women not only made up much larger portions of college classes during the seventies (they now outnumber men among college graduates) but also began to take jobs in fields that were once almost exclusively male, like law, medicine, and engineering.

Women were taking jobs that required long hours away from the home. They started refusing to quit their jobs when children were born and refusing to leave work early every time a kid got sick. Not coincidentally, many people in industrialized nations started to warn about the dangers of "the Latchkey Generation." That's what they called Gen X kids, those born between 1961 and 1981, like me.

By 1994, more than half of kids under eleven years of age had mothers in the workforce, and many people assumed that was a dangerous thing. The economist Sylvia Hewitt, who wrote the 1991 book *When the Bough Breaks: The Cost of Neglecting Our Children* said, "Child neglect has become endemic to our society."

The "latchkey crisis" became a national scandal in the United States. Voices in politics and the media shamed women who held full-time jobs, claiming their selfishness was endangering the well-being of an entire generation. Many workers responded by cutting back their hours or leaving their jobs entirely, and most of those workers were mothers.

In the 1990s, the sociologist Arlie Russell Hochschild was studying a Fortune 500 company that prided itself on its progressive work policies intended to promote a healthy work-life balance among employees and allow workers to spend plenty of time with their families. In the first chapter of the book *The Time Bind*, based on her observations at that company, she describes the home life of Gwen Bell, who worked in the PR office. While the men in the executive offices proudly boasted about being "sixty-hour men" (named after how many hours they worked a week), "Gwen's stories are more like situation comedies: stories about forgetting to shop and coming home to a refrigerator containing little more than wilted lettuce and a jar of olives, stories told in a spirit of hopeless amusement."

Gwen, like so many of her coworkers, was aware of the possibility to enroll in flex-time, or to request fewer hours. But there was an unspoken assumption that someone who worked fewer hours was not dedicated to the company and not interested in promotion. In nearly every case outlined in Hochschild's research, home life gave way to work. "The more attached we are to the world of work," the sociologist concluded, "the more its deadlines, its cycles, its pauses and interruptions shape our lives and the more family time is forced to accommodate to the pressures of work."

To be fair, very few of the employees at that company ended up using the benefits offered in order to strengthen work-life balance, which is the big surprise in Hochschild's research. Only one man chose to use his paternity leave, for example, and fewer than 3 percent of workers with young kids opted to put in part-time hours.

Most of the time, in many countries, when there are issues with a child, it is the mother who adapts her work schedule to accommodate the kid's needs and not the father. That's begun to change, but it still falls overwhelmingly on moms to handle childcare crises.

Research shows that when men watch their children, they often end up doing the more enjoyable activities, like taking kids to soccer games, while mothers tend to do more of the cleaning, cooking, and logistical management. Also, men's chore lists often include things that are done on an occasional basis, like getting oil changes for the car or mowing the lawn. Mom's list typically includes tasks that need to be done almost daily.

In a sane world, expectations of parents (and mothers especially) would have gone down when they had to spend forty or more hours at a job instead of in the home. Instead, the standards for what constitutes a good parent (at least among the working class) rose. In an op-ed called "Why Is Everyone So Busy?" staff writers at the *Economist* noted that "the rise in female employment also seems to have coincided with (or perhaps precipitated) a similarly steep rise in standards for what it means to be a good parent, and especially a good mother."

Macaroni and cheese out of a box was no longer good enough. Instead, it had to be a recipe pulled from Pinterest that uses organically sourced ingredients and promises to keep your kid's brain healthy. Grind your own coffee beans, use BPA-free plastic, supervise their internet usage, and create cute videos with your kids to share on social media.

There was simply too much to do. Instead of deciding to do less, many moms believed they could solve home problems the way they solved issues in the office. They were swayed by the appeal of efficiency and productivity in the workplace and began to bring those values into family life. More hours would mean higher quality, right? So putting in more hours with your kid would result in a happier, smarter, more successful child. No more latchkey kids. Between the years of 1986 and 2006, the number of children who said they were under surveillance at all times doubled.

While women were taking jobs at record numbers, so-called helicopter parenting began to spread throughout the United States. The term *helicoptering* was first used in a 1969 book called *Between Parent and Teenager* by Dr. Haim Ginott. It was a problem in the 1960s, but that problem has worsened in recent years, as parents have striven to *prove* their jobs are not getting in the way of being good parents. At this point, 30 percent of job recruiters say they've seen parents submit a résumé for their kid, while one in ten have had parents try to negotiate salary or benefits for their adult child.

On the surface, helicopter parenting seems to be the opposite of efficiency. It requires a larger investment of time and energy from parents. Why would someone addicted to efficiency spend *more* time doing something?

However, the goal of overparenting is to guarantee that you raise a healthy and successful child. It relies on checklists and catalogs of items your child "needs" to have a good childhood. In terms of productivity, the child is the product and the parent sometimes goes overboard in trying to make that product the best one on the market.

The cult of efficiency rests on the belief that following a rigorous schedule of activities will improve your life. In parenting, that rigorous schedule often includes debate teams and gymnastics and piano lessons and organic applesauce and top-of-the-line running shoes. It also involves doing battle for your kids and clearing obstacles that might otherwise delay them or slow them down.

A mom and dad in West Virginia filed suit against their daughter's school because she turned in her biology project late and received an F. More and more college professors say parents are contacting them to argue about their kids' grades. Some parents call their kids at college to wake them in time for their classes.

A third grade teacher told this story about an interaction with the mother of one of her students: "[She] came to my room when I was alone and tried to physically intimidate me into changing her child's grade. When I showed her the grade books and reminded her that I'd been trying to talk to her about her daughter not meeting grade-level standards, she took my grade book and put it in [her] bag, with me trailing behind her [as she] marched down to the principal's office to prove me wrong. Luckily, the principal was supportive of me, but my relationship with the parent deteriorated after that. It made it very hard to work with the little girl, who was sweet, but wasn't learning to read."

Writing your kids' book reports, arguing about their grades, and calling their teachers requires a great deal of energy and time. But it's not, I think, accomplishing what parents hope. Overparenting may feel like a good use of time, but it does not ensure success for your child. Most of the time, it does the opposite.

A large majority of current college students report feeling overwhelmed. Kids with helicopter parents are significantly more likely to suffer depression, and there's a strong link between a highly structured childhood and a lack of executive-function capabilities. Children with helicopter parents often struggle to develop self-reliance and resilience. They have simply been too often protected from adversity.

Overparenting, to me, is a classic example of a misguided strategy. It happens when a parent is determined to ensure their kid's future in what they believe is the most efficient way possible: checking those boxes on the "good childhood" list. Unfortunately, this is not just wasted time and energy. This is energy invested in accomplishing something only to find you've accomplished the opposite of what you wanted. You didn't nurture a successful adult; you made it more likely your child would not be prepared for the pressures and responsibilities of adulthood.

This discussion often becomes gendered because women assume an outsize portion of childcare duties in just about every industrialized nation. Gender also affects just about any discussion of working hours and productivity.

Many people believe the wage gap between women and men can be explained by the longer hours that men work. It's true that in the United States at least, men stay on the job for about forty minutes longer than women every week. If you include in your calculation only people working full-time, men work about 8.2 hours per day versus 7.8 for women, according to data from the U.S. Department of Labor. Keep in mind, though, that men are more likely to take breaks and go out to lunch.

If we were to compare only work habits, we might believe men are more obsessed with efficiency and productivity than women. We could conclude that men have been more affected by pressure to constantly improve than women. But that would be inaccurate once the full picture is considered. Women report spending at least an extra half hour every day on housework, whether they have children or not.

If you add in the extra time spent working on chores, the difference between the genders disappears. In fact, according to the U.S. Bureau of Labor Statistics, working moms spend eighty minutes longer every day taking care of kids and households, while dads typically spend almost fifty minutes more than moms watching TV or doing other enjoyable activities.

There are heartening improvements. Current research shows men are doing twice as much at home as they used to, but women are still taking care of the majority of household duties and childcare. In other words, men are doing more on average but are still not doing as much as their partners.

In order to accomplish all of their assigned duties, between work and home, women have doubled down on the efficient techniques they believe have helped them on the job, like multitasking and rigorous scheduling, checklists and meetings, and keeping a tight rein on the number of social activities they commit to during their off-hours.

Interestingly, India is ground central for many of the changes I'm discussing here. The rapid growth in IT jobs there, combined with new expectations that IT centers be open and responsive twenty-four hours a day, seven days a week, has put incredible pressure on all workers. The number of single parents is on the rise and nuclear families are mostly disappearing, so work-life balance has become an area of concern.

A study from two researchers at India's Anna University in 2010 found big differences between the genders in handling increased pressures at work. Apparently, when companies institute policies to strengthen work-life balance, men benefit more and see a larger decrease in stress. As the report says, "Men feel more satisfied when they achieve more on the job even at the cost of ignoring the family."

Women are not imagining the extra pressures put on them, and even if they do naturally feel more responsibility to take care of kids and home, it's impossible to tell how much of that is innate and how much is the result of centuries of gendered expectations. The end result, though, is that women struggle with a heavy weight of expectation and it's less acceptable for them to take breaks or engage in hobbies that might relieve that pressure.

A report from the *New York Times* on the "motherhood penalty" began with the following stark sentence: "One of the worst career moves a woman can make is to have children." Women, on average, take a 4 percent hit on their earnings after having a child, while men typically see a 6 percent increase, even when researchers controlled for education, experience, and hours worked.

Moms are also less likely to be hired and to be viewed as competent; the bias swings the other way for dads. One sociologist ran an experiment at Cornell in which researchers sent hundreds of fake résumés to real employers. All of the résumés were exactly the same, except that some said the applicant belonged to a PTA, implying that person was a parent.

Dads were more likely to get a callback than childless men, while the chances that a mom would get a call dropped by 50 percent. Another related study showed moms were offered the smallest salary compared to other applicants: $11,000 less than women with no kids and $13,000 less than dads.

So it's no surprise to me that women have come up with coping strategies both at work and at home, trying desperately to meet the outsize expectations placed on them. Working women are, on average, doing more work (and less enjoyable work) for less pay and less praise. What's more, when they complain about feeling overwhelmed, they're told to "lean in."

Lest it sound like I'm talking about women in general and not myself, let me assure you that I have been as prone to overscheduling as any other parent. I was a single mother for most of my son's life, and I was bound and determined to make sure that he had a good childhood regardless of my income or family status.

I would rush home from work, feeling guilty because I had to stay late to cover a press conference, pick him up from afterschool care, and rush off to the library for story time or to symphony hall for a kids' concert. I had a chart where I kept track of all his behavior and awarded him a star when he was polite all day or finished his homework before dinner.

I had plenty of work to do at home, writing scripts and editing audio interviews, but it waited until my son went to bed. I was getting five hours of sleep, on average.

One weekend, when I'd packed a picnic lunch and loaded our bikes into the car, I asked my kid what he wanted to do after visiting the park. "Can we just not go?" he asked.

I was honestly astonished. All of the trips to museums and the science center were for his benefit, not mine. When I was exhausted, I would still put a smile on my face and drag my tired self to the zoo so that he could be stimulated and not sit at home doing nothing.

When he pushed back, though, I had a flash of insight. I was trying to make sure he didn't suffer for my long hours by forcing him to put in long hours.

"I just want to do nothing," he said. "I just want to sit and play with my robots."

My son doesn't remember that exchange, but I sure do. It was a wake-up call for me, a sure sign that I'd been concerned more with my checklist than with my son's mood. We stayed home that entire weekend, watching movies, eating popcorn, and playing board games.

When it comes to obsession with productivity and efficiency, I am inclined to believe that women are more obsessed than men, in general. Women are *expected* to multitask, a habit that increases stress and is ultimately damaging to a person's cognitive abilities. At home, they are often the administrators, keeping track of toilet paper and laundry detergent, scheduling doctors' appointments and haircuts, doing the all-too-often unnoticed labor of emptying the dishwasher and folding clothes. Women are even expected to be the nurturers at work, whether they have kids or not. Women are disproportionately expected to remember birthdays, for example, and to organize parties or remember to buy coffee for the breakroom.

Unfortunately, many of the strategies we employ in order to conquer our long lists of duties are counterproductive. We may think we are practicing self-care when we limit the number of social activities we engage in, but three hours spent at home answering email and scanning social media feeds is not relaxing to the brain or body. In fact, those activities are quite stressful. Going to the coffee shop and chatting with friends for a couple hours will leave you feeling refreshed and upbeat; the time you spend surfing the web will exhaust your brain and deplete your resources.

Because we're tired, we often double down on the very habits that exhausted us in the first place: email instead of phone calls, getting up earlier in order to get things done before work, buying a new productivity journal, listening to a podcast that promises to "hack your anxiety."

I want to be clear that I'm not pointing the finger at women and saying, "What you're doing is wrong." Lord knows, the last thing any of us needs is to be shamed and blamed any more than we already are. When I talk about women who overschedule and doggedly pursue the dream of ultimate efficiency and productivity, I'm talking about myself, and I'm exhausted enough as it is. I don't need anyone telling me I need to do more.

It's not that our habits and strategies and "leaning in" are wrong, but that we tend to lose sight of what we're trying to achieve and simply focus on getting through our to-do lists. We are proud not of the ultimate goals we attain, but of how hard we are on ourselves and how many tasks we can accomplish in a single day. I asked a friend how her weekend was, and she replied that it was wonderful and then followed with a long list of all the stuff she had done. "There's only one thing left on my list," she crowed, "and I can get that done tonight. I'm almost at To-Do List Zero."

All of us, both men and women, are subject to an unnatural pressure to constantly work harder and better. We are all caught in a system that demands ever greater improvements in efficiency. It's not easy for anyone; no one gets a free pass. All workers check email on the weekends and while we're sick at home or on vacation.

I believe, however, that the system demands even more of women than it does of men. In general, men see home as a place for relaxation and look forward to the end of the workday, but for many women, the workplace is less complicated and fraught than the home. A study from 2012 found that working moms are *less* stressed than stay-at-home moms and in better health, both physically and mentally, than those who work part-time or not at all. Home is no refuge for women.

So, my advice to women is this: Be kinder to yourself. Working longer hours is not likely to bring you significant bumps in pay, but it will take a toll on your well-being. Answering emails in your off-hours is having a more damaging impact on your life than you realize, and a cupcake that has a messy smear of frosting on the top usually tastes just as good as one that is carefully decorated following a YouTube tutorial on baking.

Existing disparities in pay and promotion are not due to a lack of work on the part of women; they are the result of centuries of discrimination and bias. Fathers are more respected, mothers are less so. You will not change that by working fifty-hour weeks or keeping productivity journals; true change will require new policies and procedures.

Both men and women need to step off the treadmill that's taking us nowhere, but for women the urgency is even more intense. Lean out, ladies.

Chapter 7

DO WE LIVE TO WORK?

When John Kennedy was campaigning for the presidency, he stood one day outside a West Virginia coal mine, shaking hands with the miners as they came out with coal-blackened faces.

One miner stopped and said to Kennedy, "I understand you've never had to work a day in your life." Kennedy admitted it was true.

"You haven't missed a thing," came back the deadpan answer.

—JACK GRAHAM
A Man of God: Essential Priorities for Every Man's Life, 2007

ONE EVENING, OVER KOREAN barbecue, I explained to a friend that I was writing a book that encourages people to embrace idleness. "Oh my God," she answered, "I hate lazy people."

No, no, I quickly responded, laziness is not the same as idleness. We've simply become too attached to work, I explained, too addicted to working, and we need to balance our lives out with a little idle activity like sitting on porches or chatting with neighbors.

"I would hate that," she answered, with a moue of disgust. "I love to work. I can't stand just sitting around. Work makes me happy."

This woman, by the way, is one of the most grounded, cheerful, and talented people I know. She's also not an outlier. I've had this conversation many times over the past few years, with both friends and strangers, and I often get some version of "but I love to work" in response.

The question for me was not whether people enjoyed their work, but whether they *needed* it. That was the question that drove my research, the question I asked hundreds of people around the country, and the essential question of this book: Is work necessary?

A lot of people will disagree with my next statement, to the point of anger and outrage: Humans don't need to work in order to be happy. At this point in our historical timeline, that claim is almost subversive. The assumption that work is at the core of what it means to lead a useful life underlies so much of our morality that it may feel I'm questioning our need to breathe or eat or sleep.

But as I examined the body of research on what we know is good for all humans, what is necessary for all humans, I noted a gaping hole where work was supposed to be. This led me to ask some pointed questions about why most of us believe we can't be fully human unless we're working.

Please note that by "work" I don't mean the activities we engage in to secure our survival: finding food, water, or shelter. I mean the labor we do in order to secure everything else beyond survival or to contribute productively to the broader society, the things we do in exchange for pay.

For generations, we have been told that our life's purpose is work. Religious leaders often told the faithful that a lifetime of labor is how you earn an afterlife of respite, so idleness must be put off until after death. In truth, work ethics in the Western world have often been tied to faith, especially in the United States.

In 1901, the Episcopal bishop of Massachusetts told parishioners, "To seek for and earn wealth is a sign of a natural, vigorous, and strong character." (He was a good friend of J. P. Morgan, by the way. At the moment the bishop spoke these words, Morgan was helping him raise $5 million for his church.)

For centuries now, the Protestant faith has been among the most vigorous in declaring the virtue of work and the shamefulness of even short periods of idleness. This emphasis has become so embedded in our psyches that research shows emotional trauma caused by unemployment is actually 40 percent more severe among Protestants.

The economics professor Davide Cantoni studied this phenomenon and concluded that while Protestantism doesn't make you wealthier, money doesn't seem to be the point. "Work becomes the object in itself," Cantoni concluded.

This idea has been confirmed by other researchers. The University of Pennsylvania professor Alexandra Michel says people put in long hours not for "rewards, punishments, or obligation" but because "many feel existentially lost without the driving structure of work in their life—even if that structure is neither proportionally profitable nor healthy in a physical or psychological sense."

This could be a strong argument for a biological imperative, that our drive to work hard is innate and overrides other considerations not connected with monetary reward. It's certainly a tendency that we in the industrialized world have passed on to our children. In a *Washington Post* piece, Rachel Simmons of Smith College recounted something a college sophomore once told her: "I can't have downtime. I feel like I'm doing something wrong if I'm not doing anything." All of this evidence could lead us to believe that working is not a choice, but a need.

Some have even made a convincing argument that human beings cannot bear to be idle. Christopher Hsee and his colleagues carried out a series of studies in which they gave people the option between doing something and doing nothing and it turned out that people felt better when they did something. The report went so far as to say that "idleness is potentially malignant."

Let's consider that for a moment, then. Is work necessary for human happiness? Do we work hard because to do otherwise would be unhealthy?

There's no doubt that many cultures share a contempt for people who lounge around while their neighbors toil. Aesop's cautionary tale about the grasshopper and the ant is meant to warn us that if we spend too much time enjoying ourselves, we'll die. Laziness is an unattractive quality in most people's eyes and we have lots of derogatory names for idlers: layabouts, bums, slackers, sluggards, good-for-nothings.

There are some very smart thinkers who believe work is what gives our life meaning because without it we accomplish nothing and make no mark upon history. Without work, we might die and it would be as though we had never lived. Since evolution is fueled by a desire to leave a lasting legacy, this argument can be quite compelling. Elon Musk once wondered how people could find meaning without a job. "A lot of people derive meaning from their employment," he warned. "If you're not needed, what is the meaning? Do you feel useless?"

It seems the answer to his question might be yes. In the United States, the number of people still working past retirement age has risen by almost 35 percent in recent years. One in ten baby boomers say they don't plan on ever retiring.

It goes without saying that there are practical explanations for this trend. Average life expectancy has gone up in most nations, and seniors need a lot more money in order to support themselves through decades of retirement. Plus, a global recession in the early twenty-first century eroded the savings of millions of seniors and forced many to go back to the workplace.

But there are deeper, less tangible reasons behind the decision by so many to continue working. As Ann Brenoff wrote on *HuffPost,* "I don't know *how* to retire. While I never thought of how to retire as something that needed to be learned or taught, perhaps it is. . . . What will [I] do when the alarm clock no longer rings each morning?"

This is the existential crisis that many of the post–World War II generation are now facing. They have spent their lives focused on their work. Their homes and very identities are tied up in what they have done for a living. So what happens to your identity when its defining characteristic disappears? Baby boomers are known for their work ethic and were motivated for decades by a drive to constantly get ahead. What happens when that drive is suddenly thrown into neutral?

It certainly makes it difficult to answer one of the most common questions in the United States: "What do you do?"

That question is considered rude in many other countries but is often one of the first things Americans want to know about others, mostly because knowing someone's profession makes it easier to categorize them and rank them.

It should come as no surprise that the connection between employment and identity can be traced back to the dawn of the industrial age. Prior to that time, people were more likely to ask about a person's family than about their job.

If you've been told for more than half a century that hard work is patriotic, that it is what separates a good person from a contemptible person, and that labor is part of the dues one must pay in order to earn entrance to heaven, what might happen when that labor ends and your life continues?

It's not just seniors who feel the undertow of the workplace, and they are certainly not the only ones who are uncomfortable with unemployment. Many people crave work and are uncomfortable in its absence, even during short vacations. All of this could be seen as evidence that work is an inherent human need.

There is yet another reasonable explanation for hard work: Progress requires it. We would have no great achievements in science or art, of course, had some not invested Malcolm Gladwell's recommended 10,000 hours to attain mastery. Imagine the labor involved in building Machu Picchu, for example, or the Great Wall of China, the hours that Marie Curie spent in her lab, or the decades during which Beethoven slaved at his piano.

Hard work, in this view, is good because it is the only way to improve your life and the lives of those around you. "Hard work is the only way forward," the Harvard economist Richard

Freeman advised. "There is so much to learn and produce and improve that we should not spend more than a dribble of time living as if we were in Eden. Grandchildren, keep trucking."

It's quite true that having important work to do can lead to a mood boost. In fact, a survey of 485 separate studies demonstrated conclusively that people who like their work are more likely to be healthy in body and mind. Also, they are less likely to suffer from anxiety and depression than those who are either unemployed or who don't like their jobs. Research commissioned by the United Kingdom also showed the damage caused by *not* having a job outweighs the stress of having one. In another study, the sociologist Sarah Damaske undertook a research project intended to determine whether people who work are less stressed while at work than they are at home. Turns out, people are often more relaxed in the office. Damaske explained in an interview that even the most urgent of issues at work is not as stressful as a crisis at home. Missing a deadline, for example, doesn't usually take the same toll as the death of a loved one.

What's more, Damaske says, we always have an escape option in our working lives that we may not have at home. "You still know that you can quit, you can look for something else, that you can leave—leave your boss and your bad day behind," Damaske said. Most people don't walk out on their families because they've become irritating or find a new family when the old one is causing anxiety. You are usually tied to your family in ways that you're not shackled to your job.

This is all compelling, but ultimately unconvincing. When defending the idea that work is necessary for human happiness, some point to research that shows people live longer if they have a sense of purpose. I find that argument irrelevant, since one's purpose does not have to be tied up with one's job.

Stay-at-home parents, for example, can have an incredibly strong sense of purpose. Vincent van Gogh was basically unemployed. He sold only one painting during his lifetime, and yet his lack of financial success never weakened his sense of purpose or dedication to his art.

Still, we know that for every extra year a person works, their chance of suffering dementia drops by 3 percent.

Unemployment can also take a severe toll on a person's psyche, and not just because of worries over money (although those are significant for most people). Even when controlling for loss of income, going without a job can be psychologically damaging. Many people in the industrialized world derive self-esteem from their jobs. Jobs confer status. It can be devastating to feel unwanted and useless.

But does all this mean that work is a fundamental human need? Do we require productive work in order to remain healthy and viable? If we were supplied with food, water, shelter, and clothing, would we still need to work in order to thrive?

My answer is no. I think the benefits conveyed by a meaningful career may stem from the value and emphasis placed on work by our culture, not by nature. I think it's stressful to be unemployed because most of us live paycheck to paycheck and because we lose status among our family and friends when we don't have a job title.

At heart, I believe work is a tool that can be used to fulfill other needs, but is not a requirement in and of itself. Consider this updated list of human needs, posited by the neuroscientist Nicole Gravagna:

1. Food
2. Water
3. Shelter
4. Sleep
5. Human connection
6. Novelty

While most of us need to work a certain number of hours to attain the first three, none of those six things absolutely require labor.

There are many examples of people who've been relieved of a need to work, and they are no more unhealthy than the rest of us. Men who don't work are not more likely to abuse alcohol or get a divorce. They're also not at higher risk of dying compared to their cohorts who have full-time jobs. After all, Thoreau died from tuberculosis, not because he chose to spend a couple years in a cabin by a quiet pond.

The question, for me, is not about whether work is necessary or good. For the vast majority of the population, that question is moot, because some kind of gainful employment is required in order to survive. The real question is whether we can survive without work, and we very definitely can. Most of us would be fine if we inherited $25 million tomorrow and spent the rest of our lives watching movies and gardening.

If the vast majority of us have to work some hours in order to survive, then the better question becomes: Must we work as long and hard as we do? The historical record shows that prior to the Industrial Revolution, our workdays lengthened and shortened according to the difficulty of the task at hand, not according to an arbitrary measure like the clock. Historians have noted that before the age of manufacturing, our lives alternated between periods of intense labor, like a harvest, and expansive rest, like the celebration after a harvest.

For the most part, this pattern has held, even through the past two hundred years, for the lucky few who work for themselves. If you sift through historical documents, you'll find that some of the most productive minds of the nineteenth and twentieth centuries worked only about four hours a day. Charles Darwin, Ingmar Bergman, Charles Dickens, and the incredibly prolific mathematician Henri Poincaré all worked for just a small portion of each day.

The artist Caravaggio reportedly partied for a month every time he finished a piece. While he was working on *Madame Bovary,* Gustave Flaubert put in about five hours each day writing, and spent the rest of the day reading, strolling with family members, talking with his mother, enjoying a bit of chocolate, smoking a pipe, and taking a hot bath. The novelist Thomas Mann wrote for only about three hours a day.

Consider the research into ants that's being conducted at Georgia Tech. Scientists there spent many hours watching fire ants in order to learn something about efficiency. After all, what creature is more organized, efficient, and productive than an ant? Researchers expected to find a busy group of insects, with every member of the colony digging and hauling and working hard.

Instead, they discovered that Aesop got the ant all wrong when he wrote his fable about the grasshopper. In fact, only a small group of ants in the colony did most of the work, while the others hung out and stayed out of the way. Crowding too many ants into the tunnel where they were working impeded progress. In fact, allowing some ants to focus on digging while others were idle accomplished the most while expending the least amount of energy. "If you look at energy consumed, lazy is the best course," concluded Daniel Goldman, a professor in the School of Physics at Georgia Tech.

I'm not saying you should take life lessons from fire ants, but I do think this is a demonstration of how natural *and efficient* idleness can be. This is also a good moment to take stock of how damaging our work ethic is at times. It's not the emphasis on hard work that's toxic, but the obsession with it. We now live in a culture in which we are not happy *being* and only satisfied when we're *doing*.

Maintaining that kind of guiding principle has unintended consequences. For one thing, it makes us less compassionate. For example, when Protestants are prompted to think about their jobs, they experience an immediate decrease in their empathy. (Remember that Protestants are among the most likely to believe hard work is its own reward.)

This connection between thinking about work and empathy needs to be further investigated, I think, because now that we carry our inboxes around with us, we think about work all the time. Is it possible that the recent decline in empathy around the world is due at least in part to the fact that our phones serve as constant reminders of our jobs?

There's no denying that hard work helped build nations and the global economy. It's hard to view the Industrial Revolution as anything other than an economic success, but it's misguided to believe that work is anything other than a tool to achieve other goals. Emerson said that "beauty is its own excuse for being," but that's not true of labor. Labor needs a reason.

A number of businesses have experimented with shorter hours and had incredible results. In 2018, a large estate planning company based in New Zealand decided to experiment with a shortened workweek. Employees put in only four days but were paid for five. At the end of the trial period, leadership scores rose by double digits, as did engagement.

The number of people at the firm who said they were managing the work-life balance well increased by 26 percent, stress went down, and motivation went up. The company's founder, Andrew Barnes, decided to make the policy permanent. He told the *NZ Herald,* "We're not focusing on the right thing. We're focusing on the days and therefore the assumption is the days deliver the amount worked, but this doesn't always hold true." Barnes found that although hours worked are easy and inexpensive to track, they may not provide the best measure to evaluate employee performance.

I decided to test this for myself. Could I get the same amount of work done in fewer hours? For a full month, I took note of what time I started work in the morning. I took a short break every fifty minutes or so to walk the dog or water the plants and create a bit of distance between myself and the task at hand. However, I made sure that I focused on what I was doing by muting my phone and closing my email and any other open tabs in my browser.

I also took off my watch and used a Post-it to cover the clock on my computer so I wouldn't know how much time had passed. My intention was to stop using the arbitrary measure of the number of hours spent at my desk and instead become more attuned to my inner clock.

When I found myself struggling to focus and becoming restless, I stepped away from my desk, found a clock, and noted down the time. After thirty days had passed, I totaled my work hours. On most days, I put in four hours and ten minutes of focused work. My longest single stint was about six hours and my shortest was two and a half. In general, I need no less than a full day off each week, sometimes two, in which I do no work whatsoever and ignore my email. When I didn't get that time to rest, I struggled to focus and was much more easily distracted.

My sample size is one, but it's a useful experiment to carry out in your own life. I proved to myself that I don't need forty to sixty hours a week of focused work. In fact, despite a drastic cut in hours, I'd been more productive by the end of the thirty days. On average, I write about 1,000 words a day, respond to 54 emails and messages, and read about 400 pages of research. During the time when I was not watching the clock but focusing on my tasks until I couldn't focus any longer, I wrote an incredible 1,600 words a day and read about 550 pages. My email numbers stayed about the same.

Some industries don't see the same benefits from fewer hours, of course. A small start-up called Treehouse experimented with a thirty-two-hour workweek in 2015 and by the next year had abandoned that policy. In fact, many employees were working sixty hours a week by late 2016. It's impossible to know, without further study, why fewer hours work in some companies and not in others, but the majority of accounts I've found show curtailing hours results in no loss of productivity and a gain in emotional and physical health among workers.

The bottom line is that work is not always good and healthy. According to data from the United Nations, work kills more than twice as many people annually than war does and more than both drugs and alcohol combined.

So if we see health benefits from working, it could be because of tenets that have been drilled into our heads to make us feel ashamed for being idle. We feel better when we're working because society tells us we should feel bad if we're not.

It's like being told for years that popcorn is healthy and that upstanding people eat lots of it, so you eat nothing but popcorn and get sick. We were told that we need work to live, that work is never wrong, and so we are overdosing.

If too much work causes harm, that probably means a reasonable amount of idleness is healthy and that well-being demands a balance between labor and leisure. That's a fair summary of Idle Theory. Idle Theory posits that we make ourselves weaker by working too hard and that lazier creatures have an evolutionary advantage.

Every living being has to do some work in order to stay alive, of course. According to Idle Theory, the entities that meet their survival needs with the least amount of work are most likely to survive. Chris Davis, one of the original proponents of this theory, calls it "Survival of the Idlest."

This echoes an old quote often misattributed to Bill Gates that suggests that when there's a tough job to be done, it's best to look for the laziest workers because they'll find the easiest way to get it done. It appears that sentiment was first expressed by a Chrysler executive named Clarence Bleicher. He testified before a Senate committee in 1947 and said: "The lazy man will find an easy way to do it. He may not do much, but he will find an easy way to do it. . . . That has been my experience." That comment has rung so true that it's survived for a half century and been attributed to a number of business executives besides Bill Gates.

Idle Theory suggests that placing a value on laziness is not just a good corporate strategy but a solid evolutionary one. And there are some who even say laziness is the underlying motivation beneath a great deal of innovation. "The first person who thought of putting a sail on a boat wanted to get out of rowing. Whoever hitched a plow to an ox was looking for a way to escape digging. Whoever harnessed a waterfall to grind grain hated pounding it with rocks," wrote Fred Gratzon in his 2003 book *The Lazy Way to Success.* One might even say the Industrial Revolution began when a Scotsman figured out he could plug a loom into an engine and avoid driving horses in a circle all day.

Darwin believed existence is a war and the strong prevail. If you buy in to Idle Theory, existence is actually a struggle to be idle and the most successful, like lions, balance intense periods of activity with hours spent lounging in the sun of sub-Saharan Africa.

Idleness in this view is not inactivity. It's not sitting like a lump and doing nothing. Remember that fishermen are often idle while working, as are cooks and security guards. They are inactive while at work and active in their off-work hours. That's why it's wrong to use idleness as a synonym for laziness.

Idleness is really time in which one is not actively pursuing a profitable goal. It means you are at leisure. There is considerable scientific research demonstrating that idleness is good for you. There is even a good deal of clinical study that suggests idleness is associated with high intelligence. One study at Florida Gulf Coast University discovered a link between a lack of activity and deeper thinkers, although the sample size was incredibly small (only sixty students).

That may not have been an aberrant finding, though. Another study showed that people who worked about fifty-five hours a week scored lower on cognitive tests than those who worked about forty. Decades of research demonstrate that we are more creative, more insightful, and generally sharper when we allow ourselves a significant amount of leisure time. It makes sense, too, when you think back to times in your life when you worked a considerable amount of overtime. Do you think you were in the right frame of mind then to think creatively or carefully?

I think the weight of scientific opinion shows that a certain amount of idleness is required in order for the human brain to function best. Although we think of great men and women as hard workers, many of them were as rigorous about scheduling leisure as they were about getting things done. As Alex Soojung-Kim Pang, author of *Rest: Why You Get More Done When You Work Less*, writes: "Darwin and Lubbock, and many other creative and productive figures, weren't accomplished despite their leisure; they were accomplished because of it."

One of the tragic consequences of rising smartphone usage is the death of boredom. In our hours of leisure, we used to experience some measure of ennui from time to time, but we are rarely bored these days, and the younger generation almost doesn't know the meaning of the word. This is not a good development because boredom is an inherently fertile state of mind.

It's true that we don't enjoy boredom. That's what makes it valuable, though, because when we feel bored, our brains are strongly motivated to find a meaningful occupation. Thoughts are not directed or controlled and are therefore free to travel in unexpected directions. "Once you start daydreaming and allow your mind to wander," says the psychologist Sandi Mann, author of *The Upside of Downtime: Why Boredom Is Good,* "you start thinking beyond the conscious and into the subconscious."

When our minds are allowed to relax and rest, they return to what's called the "default network." This is the part of the brain that sorts through all the new information we've received recently and tries to put it into context with what we already know. The default network is integral to learning, insight, and imagination. If our minds never come to rest, there is never an opportunity to wander into new directions.

Again, don't mistake rest for inactivity. When the mind is at rest, it is still active. In fact, it uses only 5 percent less energy than it does when it's focused on a task. Focus is required for directed work, but idleness is necessary for reflection.

Since reflective thought is one of the most uniquely human activities in which we engage, one of the abilities that separates us from our simian cousins, it's not much of a stretch to say that idleness helps make us more human. In fact, the neuroscientist Jonathan Smallwood thinks daydreaming "could be the crux of what makes humans different from less complicated animals."

Now you begin to see, I hope, how dangerous is the idea that we must be engaged in productive work during all of our waking hours. It's possible that too much work can separate us from our own humanity. When our minds are idle, we allow ourselves to reconnect with our creativity and reengage with reflective thought—two activities that are esssential to progress.

That is why, despite the benefits of meaningful employment, I don't believe work is a fundamental need. If we were provided with all that we needed in order to survive but were not required to work, we would be fine. We might sit by our own version of Walden Pond and think deeply about the natural world, but we would not get sick and die.

Leisure, however, does seem to be a requirement, as lack of it can make us ill. We've tipped the work-life balance in the wrong direction. At some point, we decided that working long hours was difficult, and difficulty was good for the soul, so the more you worked, the better a person you were. This is a perversion of natural human needs and abilities.

Perverse is a perfect word to describe our belief in work for work's sake. It is a perversion of what is best and most productive about humanity. Perhaps the time has come to remind ourselves of what is unique and wonderful about our species and to take stock of how and why we've left those qualities behind.

Chapter 8

UNIVERSAL HUMAN NATURE

> Why are we born free and end up enslaved?
>
> —NOAM CHOMSKY

IF WE DON'T NEED work to survive, what *do* we need? If constant work is not healthy for the human brain, what *is* healthy? What is the point, I wondered, of realizing that what I'm doing is bad for me if I don't know for sure what is good? What I needed was a how-to guide for the care of a human being, just like the books you read when you get a new pet. What do I need in order to be happy and healthy? This new line of inquiry led me to one of the most contentious debates in evolutionary biology.

Nearly half a century ago, Noam Chomsky, the linguist, social critic, cognitive scientist, and philosopher, agreed to participate in a live debate on Dutch television. In what has since become a famous dialogue, he spent about ninety minutes sparring with the French philosopher and social theorist Michel Foucault.

The two men were attempting to answer one of the most enduring questions in all of human history, the question I had about myself and my colleagues: Is there a universal human nature? Are some things bad for all humans, like chocolate for dogs, or does it always depend on the person? Are there some traits and tendencies that are common to all of us, or are we entirely shaped by culture and family? It is the question at the heart of the nature-versus-nurture dispute, and it has yet to be decisively answered.

Chomsky is a scientist, one of the founders of the study of cognitive science, and it's no surprise that he believes evolution and biology help to dictate our behavior. Foucault was fairly contemptuous of modern science, seeing it as just another method by which elites exert control over society. He rejected any suggestion that our behavior is tied to biology.

The Chomsky-Foucault debate veered fairly quickly into political territory and issues of war and oppression, but I want to stick with that question of evolution and human nature. Since that debate in 1971, we have learned much more about DNA and the workings of the mind.

The question of nature versus nurture is still an open one, but we do know that Chomsky was more right than Foucault. While we can't explain all human behavior as a product of biology, we can explain some of it. As Chomsky said almost fifty years ago, "There is something biologically given, unchangeable, a foundation for whatever it is that we do with our mental capacities."

If, as I believe, our current work habits are stripping away our humanity and it is now imperative that we return to what is natural and healthy for our species, it's essential that we first decide what that looks like. In other words, what is a natural environment for humankind? How much productivity is healthy, and at what point does the pursuit of productivity become toxic?

These are difficult but crucial questions. If some of our habits are harmful to us as a species, what do pro-human habits look like? It's not always easy to distinguish between the two. What's more, there are some who, like Foucault, reject the idea that biology determines our choices. Many of us struggle with the idea of a universal human nature. We understand that evolution helps to somewhat explain the behavior of dogs and chickens, but we refuse to apply that reasoning to humans. We are wedded to the idea of free will.

Keep in mind, very few people would argue that all our decisions and personality traits can be explained with a microscope. In the end, it's not nature *versus* nurture, but nature *and* nurture. Some of what you do is biologically based, some is a choice, some is a combination of the two. Jeffrey Schloss, a professor of natural and behavioral sciences, says we should think of it "in terms of central tendencies, not inevitabilities."

Schloss was writing for a curated discussion sponsored by the John Templeton Foundation on the topic "Does Evolution Explain Human Nature?" Nearly a dozen scientists and professors celebrated Charles Darwin's two hundredth birthday by addressing this important question. The evolutionary biologist David Sloan Wilson waxed poetic with his metaphor, saying humankind is like a musical instrument: the same basic nature but an infinite variety of songs.

Wilson is the author of *Evolution for Everyone: How Darwin's Theory Can Change the Way We Think About Our Lives.* He's part of a growing number of evolutionary biologists and psychologists who believe understanding our biological roots can help us live better lives.

His view was helpful to me as I struggled to understand my own nature and how I might move away from stress and anxiety. For me, it means understanding what I truly need in order to be healthy and fulfilled, and what I can do without. This is crucial if we are to change how we work and how we play to bring increased well-being.

A word of caution, though: Our understanding of the human mind is based almost entirely on research studies, and those studies are often flawed and not representative of the whole diaspora of human life. A survey from 2008 showed that nearly all research subjects used for studies in the top psychology journals were Western, and almost 70 percent were from the United States.

That means we are drawing conclusions about all people in the world based on the responses of a tiny percentage of them. That doesn't mean the research is unhelpful, of course, but that future investigation will be more comprehensive if it includes a diversity of people. Note that we are moving into some deep evolutionary waters. Stay with me for this, because it's fascinating and will help you to understand your behavior in a much more profound way, the same way it helped me.

So let's trace it back millions of years, to the moment when humans first split away from our chimpanzee ancestors. We don't have to go through a complicated prehistory lesson here, but the broad strokes are these: We broke away from chimps in Africa about 4 million years ago and started walking on two legs. We started using stone tools shortly after that, but the first real human didn't appear until about 2 million years ago, give or take a few hundred thousand years.

Homo sapiens didn't show up for quite a while after that. There used to be a number of human species walking around on the planet, and ours is only about 300,000 years old. (In light of this book's subject, it amused me to learn that the oldest fossils of our species were discovered lying alongside some stonework tools.) Our history is very short, in other words. Compare our 300,000 years to crocodiles, who've been around for 200 million.

Because 300,000 years is not many in evolutionary terms, it can be useful, in order to truly understand ourselves and our minds, to dig beyond the history of our own species and go back to our animal ancestors. Perhaps understanding what we have in common with our primate cousins and where we differ can lead to a better understanding of our own nature.

You may be surprised to learn just how similar we are to modern apes and chimps. Frans de Waal, one of the world's foremost primatologists, points out, "Like us, they strive for power, enjoy sex, want security and affection, kill over territory, and value trust and cooperation. Yes, we use cell phones and fly airplanes, but our psychological make-up remains that of a social primate."

We often think of our technological achievements as evidence of how much we differ from our chimp cousins, but really, our history with technology is only about 150,000 years old, a blip on the evolutionary timeline. That could mean that our current difficulties with technology are merely growing pains. Perhaps we simply haven't learned how to share space with artificial intelligence yet and at least some of our issues are caused by tech advancing so much faster than evolution.

Obviously, there are differences between chimpanzees and us. We cook our food, for example, and have sex in private. We develop advanced languages as well, and that's a very important distinction.

Apes and chimps are social creatures, like humans, but do not communicate using sophisticated language and vocabulary. Noam Chomsky points to this as evidence of a universal human nature: all humans use language, and people in two different parts of the world who have no interaction will create similar language structures.

Our natural abilities with language are also intertwined with the unique ways in which our minds work. Some biologists believe our use of language is part of the reason we are able to engage in abstract reasoning. In other words, humans may be distinguished by our ability to use scientific thinking and ask "Why?"

Perhaps we are able to think about abstract concepts like time and identity because we are able to articulate the ideas, using complicated vocabularies. We don't have to learn simply by watching. Another human can quickly and efficiently explain how to use a hammer or how to drive a car. Language has allowed us to advance in ways that other species cannot.

It's possible that our desire to pass our knowledge on to other humans is another distinguishing characteristic of our species. Language has been at the core of our success, and is perhaps the most important reason *Homo sapiens* is still around and the other human species are not. One person discovers which mushrooms are safe and which aren't and shares that information with others, thus helping to protect the entire community.

Community is an important word in this context, and it's the reason I'm focusing first on language, because our work habits have severely interfered with our ability to create communities. Language is essential and important because humans survive not alone but in groups.

Human beings are perhaps the best communicators on the planet. Conversation is our evolutionary heritage and our biological advantage. However, we evolved to share information using our voices and our ears, not using text. As of 1960, less than half of the world could read. In an incredibly short period of time, we've attempted to replace the most important platform for communication—speech—with a less advanced or efficient one—text.

The voice is an underappreciated and incredible instrument. It supplies us with data that we can get in no other way. Our ears evolved in ways that specifically help us listen better to other human voices, while our throats, mouths, and lips changed over time so that we could better speak. We evolved to talk to other humans and to hear them.

By the time a child is four to six months old, their parent can identify their cry and distinguish it from other children's with nearly 100 percent accuracy. That's how unique and expressive the human voice is. Have you ever gotten a call from a friend and only had to hear them say hi before you responded by asking, "What's wrong?"

Instantly, you somehow sense that they're upset, and that's because we have evolved to pick up on minuscule emotional gradients in a voice. Brain research shows we detect information and begin processing it less than fifty milliseconds after someone else begins to speak, and a vast amount of the information we relay to each other is sent and received subconsciously. Since text is a conscious communication tool, we can't express what the voice can because we're not even aware of what's missing.

It's confusing to me that we seek to be *more* efficient by avoiding conversation, since vocalization is so incredibly powerful to our species and, in almost every case, more efficient than text. I'd imagine that part of the reason we are wasting our time at work and putting in long, unnecessary hours is that we are neglecting to use our voices. In replacing phone calls with email and texts, we are not taking advantage of our own evolutionary inheritance.

Michael Kraus at Yale University decided to test just how expressive the human voice is. For one of his experiments, he asked people to listen to recordings of others saying the same seven words, out of context. By simply hearing strangers say words like "yellow" and "thought," participants were able to guess the speaker's educational background and employment status quite accurately. "So people were accurate, at least minimally," Kraus told WBUR, "with just hearing seven words people speak from all across the U.S."

At this point, the average office worker sends and receives about 160 emails every day. There is conflicting information out there about how we choose to communicate on our smartphones, but the most generous estimate, from eMarketer, claims we spend about fifty-five minutes a day texting and the same amount of time on the phone. It's probably no surprise that younger people spend significantly more time texting than talking, and I'm willing to bet most older people do as well.

However, voice-to-voice communication repeatedly outperforms text as more efficient and clear, so we are probably miscommunicating a lot by choosing the written word instead of the voice. And there is yet another important reason our love for texts and email is potentially problematic.

Research suggests it is our voice that humanizes us. A recent provocative study asked people to learn about others' opinions using two forms: the written word and the spoken word. It turns out that when people read a differing opinion, whether it be online or in a newspaper, they are more likely to believe the other person disagrees because the other person is stupid and doesn't understand the core concepts of the issue.

When we hear someone explain the same opinion in their own voice, we're more likely to think they disagree because they have different perspectives and experiences. On a subconscious level, we make assumptions about the other person's humanity based on the method they are using to communicate. If we're reading a blog online, we tend to think of the author as less human than ourselves. Hearing someone's voice helps us recognize them as *human* and therefore treat them in a humane way.

Your voice might go up in pitch when you're excited; your speech might slow when you're trying to be deliberate. Tiny changes in tone, rhythm, and breath, the study report says, "serve as a cue for the presence of an active mental life." Text, the researchers concluded, doesn't provide the same cues that point to a human mind behind the message. So the possibility that a reader might dehumanize the author goes way up.

It turns out, real human connection is powerful in a number of ways. For example, we know that negotiations that begin with a handshake are more likely to end successfully. Similarly, studies of brain activity show that face-to-face interaction is more likely to activate the part of the brain associated with mentalizing, or imagining the thoughts and emotions of another person. Mentalizing is the neural basis for empathy, and it's an ability that scientists believe is fairly unique to humankind.

In a carefully controlled experiment, researchers found this effect when people believed they were listening to a live speaker instead of to a recording: The part of their brain associated with imagining the thoughts and needs of others was engaged. Translation: If you think you're hearing someone speak to you, the part of your brain associated with empathy perks up, and you are more likely to feel compassionate toward that person.

This is a big part of why our overuse of email and texting is contributing to dehumanization and hatred: We simply need to hear each other's voices. Yet I've found that people have a very hard time accepting this. Globally, we have come to believe that email is more efficient, more convenient, and just better than the phone. Our addiction to email is a symptom of our obsession with efficiency and productivity. Prying people away from email is sometimes harder than taking a bone from a terrier. So let me explain it in another way that might be more convincing: neural coupling.

In 2011, scientists at Princeton University set out to learn how the human brain interacts with other human brains while communicating. They had one student tell a story about a fiasco at her high school prom, and then they asked twelve other students to listen to a recording of the tale. As the students listened, they were hooked up to an fMRI (functional magnetic resonance imaging) machine.

The researchers discovered that the brain waves of the dozen people listening to the same story began to mirror those of the storyteller. When the listeners were engaged, their brain activity was almost synchronous with that of the person talking. To me, that's such a mind-boggling result that if it hadn't really happened, I might think it was a plot point in an episode of *Star Trek*.

This phenomenon is called speaker-listener neural coupling or, more simply, "mind meld." Brain waves are essentially electrical impulses in the head. There's no good explanation for how one person's brain waves can mirror another person's, but it happens when we listen closely. In some instances, the synchronization was so strong that the listener's brain would anticipate changes in the speaker's brain by a fraction of a second. That's amazing stuff!

That kind of empathic bond cannot be duplicated by emojis. You receive information from the sound of a voice that cannot be transmitted in an email attachment. The email may feel more efficient and easier because you don't have to deal with the other person when you're writing it, but the efficiency is mostly an illusion.

I realized that my tendency to replace voice with text might be causing some of the stress and frustration I felt. This is a prime example of how understanding our essential nature can suggest tangible, practical advice: Humans communicate best through the voice, so cutting back on emails and texts will help reduce stress.

Our communication is the vehicle through which we form communities and collaborate on complicated tasks, even if someone is hearing impaired. Thus, this topic leads us directly to another essential human quality, one that is common to every member of our species: a need to belong.

If you were a zookeeper tasked with designing the perfect enclosure for your human animals, odds are you would never force them to live alone. We are a social species and we need each other. The primatologist Frans de Waal told me this: "Without a group, survival is hard, which is why belonging to a group is such a priority for all animals. They will do anything to fit in and not be ostracized, which is about as bad as getting killed." To our animal brains, social isolation equates to increased risk of death.

This drive to be a member of a group or tribe, however, goes beyond simple defense strategy or strength in numbers. We will sometimes make choices that benefit others, even at our own expense, and we share this tendency, the tendency to be generous, with our closest animal relatives. In one experiment, researchers taught monkeys to pull a chain in order to get food. Then they changed the setup so that when a monkey pulled the chain, the machine gave the animal some food but also delivered an electric shock to another monkey.

Most of the monkeys stopped pulling the chain. Some starved themselves for several days rather than injure the monkey in the next cage. This instinct became stronger, the scientists found, when the monkeys had shared a cage at one point. If they didn't know each other, they were a third less likely to forgo the food in order to protect the other. There was a natural inclination to protect their neighbors that became stronger as they grew closer. We share these protective tendencies with our simian cousins.

Humans also naturally form groups and communities and then place the needs of that community above almost all others. In a 1995 report, the psychologists Roy Baumeister and Mark Leary claimed that Freud was wrong: Sex is *not* the strongest need after survival. "Belongingness needs do not emerge until food, hunger, safety, and other basic needs are satisfied," they wrote. "But they take precedence over esteem and self-actualization."

In order for belongingness to be considered a fundamental need, a person would have to suffer some illness when the need is not met. That is true in this case. Lack of belonging and social isolation are quite devastating to the human mind and body. Research has shown that having a rich social life makes you less likely to get cancer or suffer a heart attack. People who belong to a community live longer, experience less stress, and are more likely to say their lives are meaningful.

Loneliness can lead to ill health and even death, and, as it turns out, the negative impacts of social isolation are tied back to our need to belong. That need is primal. Not only can it be disastrous when the need is not met, but it's very beneficial when it *is* met. Consider an experiment conducted in 2005.

Forty-two married couples between the ages of twenty-two and seventy-seven were given small blister wounds on their arms. (I know. I'm also surprised at what people are willing to do in order to further scientific knowledge.) It turns out, the couples who admitted there was hostility in their marriages took nearly twice as long to heal as those with supportive partners. In other words, being part of a healthy marriage or partnership can help your body heal.

This phenomenon has been noted in many studies from all over the globe. Social contact (provided it's not hostile) can reduce pain and strengthen the immune system. The surgeon and author Atul Gawande says, "Without sustained social interaction, the human brain may become as impaired as one that has incurred a traumatic head injury." That sounds like a fundamental need to me.

Belonging to a social group has helped our species almost from the first appearance of *Homo sapiens* on the planet. Not only does it keep us safer and allow us to collaborate in order to take down much larger animals, like buffalo and lions, but it also seems to have made us smarter. There's good evidence that the rigors of dealing with other people (people can be tough to handle, right?) forced our brains to expand. Apes who belong to larger communities, for example, have larger brains than those who are more isolated.

The need to belong may have originated, many millions of years ago, as an efficient method to protect a species that was physically outmatched by many of its animal neighbors and by its human relatives like Neanderthals. Since then, this need has fundamentally changed our brains and our bodies so that we now can't flourish without becoming a member of a healthy social group.

That doesn't mean we have to like each other all the time in order to be healthy. Competition and argument are both natural within social groups. There is a line, though. If the competition goes too far, or the argument becomes aggressive, it can be harmful. Hostility is what determines the difference between healthy and not, so that interaction that is overwhelmingly angry or aggressive is probably not good for you.

Let's bring this discussion back to practicality for a moment. Since belonging is a fundamental need, seeking out isolation is not good for you. And yet, more and more of us are avoiding other people and think it's more efficient to work from home and order delivery of our meals, our groceries, our pet supplies, and anything else we can get without going to the store. Seeking out isolation may be at the heart of our rising stress. It is certainly not doing us any good.

Quality social interaction isn't just good for you—it's essential. The need to belong underlies many of our best impulses. It is probably what underlies empathy, for example, and empathy is a crucial component of human life.

Frans de Waal tells the story of a Russian scientist who was caring for a young chimpanzee. At one point, the chimp climbed onto the roof and the scientist couldn't get him down. She tried calling to him and luring him with fresh fruit, but he wouldn't budge. In the end, she pretended to hurt herself and then sat on the ground crying. At last, the chimp came down and embraced her, choosing to give up his perch only in order to console his friend. "The empathy of our closest evolutionary relatives exceeds even their desire for bananas," de Waal writes.

Empathy in service of belonging may be the underpinning of our basic moral code. You'll find a version of the golden rule in almost every major religion in history: Do unto others as you'd have them do to you.

Yet it requires a measure of empathy in order to do for others what we want for ourselves. It requires that we put ourselves in their place and wonder how they would want to be treated. " 'Love thy neighbor,' interpreted from an evolutionary point of view," writes the paleontologist Simon Conway Morris, "is an algorithm for social connectedness. The touted virtues of chastity, moderation, compassion, diligence, patience, moral commitment, and humility provide touchstones for effective group action."

Darwin was confused by altruism. He couldn't quite explain it from an evolutionary standpoint and ended up arguing that it must be transactional, that we give to others in the expectation that we'll get something in return. That may be true in some cases, but I don't think it fully explains human generosity and selflessness.

I believe empathy often motivates altruism. We see another person suffering and can imagine how painful it would be if our situations were reversed, and so we offer help. Empathy strengthens social bonds and helps to foster social inclusion, which makes it crucial in helping us fulfill our need to belong.

There's good reason to believe that we are now pursuing strategies and habits that contribute to a decline in empathy, though we are not aware our habits are having that effect. For example, the medical community has been working for years to figure out why so many doctors and nurses lose empathy for their patients and where the decline begins. It turns out, the decline begins in medical school and may be the result of curriculum. In an effort to train professionals more efficiently, many schools now emphasize emotional detachment.

As a result, declines in empathy have been recorded during *the first year* of medical school, before clinical practice and before medical professionals have seen enough injury and death to become hardened to them. That suggests schools may be efficient at teaching physicians about anatomy and medical technology, but not effective in teaching them how to see their patients as human beings with complex inner perspectives and experiences.

Empathy is crucial for the survival of our species, and so it is almost universally innate in humans. Babies as young as seven months old can form empathic bonds with others. One study monitored babies' brains as the children watched other people touching. Seeing a person touch the back of another's hand activated the same area in the child's brain, as though the child had felt a touch on his or her own hand. We are born, it seems, with the ability to form unspoken bonds with other humans.

If we lose that ability as adults, it's because we are not exercising it enough or are participating in activities that cause its decline. Remember that our empathy is not stirred by emails and text messages as strongly as it is by hearing another voice. That makes it all the more important that we begin to construct workplaces that involve in-person and over-the-phone interactions, and that help meet our need to belong, without impinging on the social groups people have outside the office.

We'll get into the specifics about how to address some of these issues later, though. Let's get back to what we know about human nature and what it can teach us about what we need in order to maintain well-being. We need to hear voices, we need to belong, and we need to feel empathy for one another in order to banish hostility from our relationships. We also need rules.

If you're thinking of early humans as primitive flower children who just did what they wanted all day, you may be surprised to discover that humans have a primal love for rules. We like structure and habits and routine. As the anthropologist Robin Fox says, "It's the most basic feature of human nature. We're the rule-making animal."

We are tribal, of course, but also territorial. We like to create guidelines for who is a member of the tribe and who isn't, where we live and where we don't. Just about every society in history has placed restrictions on when one human can take the life of another, for example. Sometimes those restrictions are included in the larger message of a spiritual practice, sometimes they aren't, but they're always created and enforced.

It certainly makes sense that a species that survives through cooperation would need rules in order to govern behavior. Good fences, in this sense, really do make good neighbors. The impulse to follow the rules is deeply embedded in our psyches, and that's mostly a good thing.

Having rules allows us to coexist in peace. One scientist pointed out to me that apes would never be able to gather with other unknown apes simply for the purpose of entertainment. "Chimps," Frans de Waal says, "would fight." Yet we regularly gather by the thousands for concerts and parades, and we get along because we sit in our assigned seats and stand behind the yellow lines and stop talking when the music starts. We get along because we know and follow the rules. We have centuries of evolution urging us to follow social norms. Some people resist that urge, but most don't.

So that's another basic need for humans that, so far as we know, is universal: rules. This is clearly practical knowledge, since it means that it is both natural and healthy to establish boundaries and limits and to create structures. There are two last behaviors that appear to be common to all members of our species, across geography and history: music and play.

The earliest musical instrument was almost certainly the human voice, accompanied by slapping the knees or stamping the feet, but scientists have discovered flutes made of ivory and bone that date back more than 42,000 years.

Music probably serves an important evolutionary purpose. Many researchers believe music helped *Homo sapiens* get the upper hand against Neanderthals. Because it is so effective at building communities and strengthening empathy, music was probably instrumental (pardon the pun) in creating broad social networks and relaying information. Believe me, I'm not just saying this because I'm a musician. I'm biased, but that doesn't make it less true.

Play serves an important function as well, which is likely why it's common to all human cultures. Of course, anyone who's spent time around a dog or watched squirrels for any length of time knows we're not the only ones who play. Just as wrestling dogs are honing their coordination, balance, and athletic abilities, so are small humans while playing tag.

Play helps us develop socially, physically, and cognitively. It can also teach us how to handle unexpected events. Playing games teaches young children about social rules and establishes bonds within a community. It helps us create trust and manage stress. The ecologist Marc Bekoff, who worked with Jane Goodall, says that when we are playing, "we are most fully human."

Many other things, like work, have been described as inherent human needs, but these I've listed are the only ones that seem to be consistent across cultures and across generations. These are the essential qualities of a human being: social skills and language, a need to belong that fosters empathy, rule-making, music, and play. We excel at these things, and we need them in order to be healthy.

I compared that list with my current work habits and it became immediately clear that I was not creating an environment or a schedule that allowed space for those activities. The only one I seemed to be enthusiastic about was rule-making. I make all kinds of rules for myself, like waking up early and going to the gym and tweeting enough to grow my brand. There was nothing in the schedule related to music or play or increasing my empathy.

Remember, evolution simply cannot fully explain our behavior. One of the enduring mysteries is why we consistently choose to do things that hurt us and hurt our communities, not unknowingly like a dog eating chocolate with no understanding of the consequences, but with full knowledge, as when we smoke cigarettes. We do bad stuff, and we know it's bad. I can't explain why.

One definition of goodness is something that helps our species survive and thrive. I think one of the strongest arguments that biology doesn't explain all of human nature is our irrationality. We do things that are not good for us. Regularly.

One of the most dangerous examples of this is our tendency to deny our need to belong by isolating ourselves from authentic human contact. Current teenagers are spending significantly less time with friends than teens in the twentieth century. My generation, Gen X, hung out with friends for about an hour longer than current high school seniors do.

We have already received warnings that this trend is connected to a rise in loneliness and depression. The alarm started going off years ago and the problem is expected to reach epidemic proportions within a decade or so. We have mostly ignored that warning and leaned in to the habits that are isolating us and making us sick.

We are like a patient who's diagnosed with lung cancer but decides to increase the number of cigarettes they smoke. Yes, it's that dire. Loneliness and social isolation increase a person's risk of death by 25 to 30 percent. We have a fundamental need to belong, a hunger for community, and we are choosing to starve ourselves.

Instead of investing our time in group activities like clubs or other hobby-focused groups, we are pouring our time into our jobs and into never-ending individual self-improvement schemes. But work is not a fundamental need, while community is.

I can testify based on my own experience, because I've made drastic changes as a result of what I've learned and I'm happier and healthier because of those changes. I will make even more in the years ahead.

This is what makes the issue of productivity versus idleness so very urgent. At the moment, we are self-destructive. It's essential that we remember what is most fundamental to our species and return to a lifestyle that meets our primal needs. "Just because we have a capacity for change," says the evolutionary biologist David Sloan Wilson, "does not mean that we will necessarily change for the better. Evolution frequently results in outcomes that are highly undesirable for long-term human welfare."

In a short span of about two hundred years, we have stepped far away from human nature and tried to push ourselves further toward digital existence and isolation. This will hurt us in the long run if we can't learn to limit our use of these tools. Not eliminate them, but accept reasonable limits. Noam Chomsky once said that "humans may well be a nonviable organism." He was talking about our propensity to destroy the planet; I think his words also apply to our propensity to destroy ourselves.

A return to our own basic humanity is overdue. It is now a question not of preference but of survival.

Chapter 9

IS TECH TO BLAME?

> As for all those time-saving gizmos, many people grumble that these bits of wizardry chew up far too much of their days, whether they are mouldering in traffic, navigating robotic voice-messaging systems or scything away at email—sometimes all at once.
>
> —"WHY IS EVERYONE SO BUSY?"
> *The Economist, December 2014*

WITH THE DAWNING REALIZATION that I was overscheduled, overly obsessed, and overwhelmed came a curiosity about where this started in my life. I wasted plenty of time as a kid, so how did I transform from the college student who lay next to her bookshelf rereading her favorite Agatha Christie novels to a perpetually exhausted professional who told others she didn't have time to read fiction?

The first, most obvious culprit was the smartphone in my hand. I didn't call friends and ask for restaurant recommendations anymore because I could choose a place based on how many stars it had on Yelp. I didn't have to lie down next to my bookcase to read books—I could load them onto my Kindle and read ten minutes at a time while waiting at the subway stop or sitting in my doctor's waiting room.

It's not just my smartphone, either. There's a laptop computer sitting on my desk that draws me like a magnet and keeps a firm hold during all the hours I used to spend working on my hobbies or calling my friends to see if they wanted to come over.

Clearly, I thought, the problem must be technology. The Digital Revolution has changed all of our lives, perhaps irrevocably, and the solution to our efficiency addiction is simple: Dump the phone. *All I can do is become a neo-Luddite,* I thought. Trade in the smartphone for a flip phone that can't download apps or play podcasts; establish strict limits on my computer use so I get my work done and then get up from the desk without getting pulled down the rabbit hole of clickable links; turn off my Wi-Fi when I'm not actively working.

I did all of those things. I spent three weeks without using an app on my phone except for GPS. I watched live TV instead of Netflix, which was disconcerting. I listened to CDs instead of my music service. I called people instead of texting, and I limited my time on the computer to five hours a day. I took off my Fitbit and dug my old Timex out of the box where I'd stored it years ago. It was 1995 in my house for the better part of a month.

It didn't work.

After three weeks of analog life, I was still overbooked, overwhelmed, and constantly looking for more efficient ways to spend my time. I had slowed down a little, by necessity, only because my tech made it easier to indulge my addiction to productivity. But when I took away the tech, the addiction was still there.

If tech wasn't my problem, maybe it's not the source of the wider problem. It's possible that tech is not causing the cultural changes that are so unhealthy for us. I set out to answer this question: Is technology to blame?

Sadly, the answer is more complicated than a simple yes or no. Let's not forget that there's nothing unnatural about technology. Is it unnatural for an otter to use a rock to crack open an oyster? For a beaver to build a dam, or an octopus to use coconut shells as a kind of armor? Chimps and gorillas use tools, as do crows and rats and many other creatures. Elephants have been known to craft fly swatters out of branches and drop logs onto electric fences in order to avoid injury.

Human beings have been using tools and technology since at least the Stone Age. Tech has been crucial to our survival. Too cold? We created clothes. Need to cook? We created pots. Need to carry water? We fashioned bottles and leather bags. Research even shows that when we pick up tools, our brains treat them as extensions of our bodies. Grab a hammer and the mind behaves as though that hammer is part of your arm. That's how natural tools and other technology are.

There's a crucial difference, though, between the tools we've used for thousands of years and the technology of today. When you finish pounding a nail into a board, you generally set the hammer down, and when you're done boiling water in a pot, you put the pot away. Most of the time, we use tools to accomplish specific tasks over limited periods of time, but that's not how we use our smartphones. With our phones, the task is never complete, and so the tool is never put away.

Let's get the bad news out of the way first. Let's lay out all the reasons why our tech can be harmful, and I must warn you: It's a long list.

When I ask my friends to imagine life without a smartphone, most stare at me blankly in complete confusion. One friend says she has left her car keys at restaurants, her dog at the park, and her wallet at an airport security line, but usually knows within seconds if she doesn't have her phone. How quickly these devices became indispensable! Remember, we lived without smartphones for many more years than we've lived with them.

Smartphones are an extremely recent development. The first real smartphone was the Nokia 9000 Communicator, introduced in 1996 for about $800 (that would equal about $1,300 in 2019). BlackBerrys came around in 1999, at a time when only about 60 percent of American adults had a cell phone of any kind. Owning a BlackBerry in 2005 was still considered cool.

The iPhone came out in 2007. A few years later, in 2011, just 35 percent of us had smartphones, according to data from Pew Research. By 2018, that percentage was near 80 percent. Stop for a moment and really think about all this. It's been just a few years since the majority of adults started using smartphones, but we've quickly become addicted to them.

After I left my wallet at home one day and ended up at the airport with no ID, I bought a phone wallet so I can keep my ID and cards with the phone that I know, no matter what, I will not forget. If I'm addicted, I reasoned, I might as well let that addiction work in my favor.

Most people touch their phones about 2,600 times between waking and sleeping and spend about five hours browsing on them every day. Consider that when you're feeling pressed for time. Out of a twenty-four-hour day, you probably spend about six to seven hours sleeping and eight hours at work. That leaves just nine hours, and you spend more than half of that time staring at your phone. Eighty-five percent of us use them while chatting with our family and friends. I probably don't even need to prove this point, since more than half of Americans admit they're addicted to their phones.

"I think a lot about how jobs used to be structured around smoke breaks or chats around the water cooler," Jared Yates Sexton of Georgia Southern University said to me. "We've now structured our jobs around that phone." It boggles my mind to consider how rapidly these phones became ubiquitous in our lives and how thoroughly they've changed our habits, our lifestyles, and even our brains.

First and foremost, cell phones have changed the way we communicate with one another, mostly for the worse. The irony for me is that we choose not to talk to people because we actually believe emails and texting are more efficient, which couldn't be further from the truth. Perhaps the most significant cause of our overuse of technology is an underlying belief that digital methods are always superior to analog options. Our drive to always increase productivity (we never stop to wonder if there's a limit to how much we can produce) sends us back, time and again, to the computers on our desks and the phones in our hands.

While beefing up computing power has a measurable impact on our laptops, that's not how it works for the human brain. You can't upgrade your gray matter and expect it to work faster. Our brains do not function like computers, and therefore we should never measure ourselves against the speed of a digital processor. And yet that's exactly what we do. When computers were introduced into the workplace, they sped up many processes that had originally been designed for human rhythms.

Remember that in post–industrial age society, time is money, so faster processing speeds can generate more profits more quickly. But humans can't keep up. "The computer introduces a time frame in which the nanosecond is the primary temporal measurement," writes the social theorist Jeremy Rifkin. "The nanosecond is a billionth of a second, and though it is possible to conceive theoretically of a nanosecond . . . *it is not possible to experience it.* Never before has time been organized at a speed beyond the realm of consciousness." Meaning that while the computers calculate at incredible speeds, the brain needs to go slower. Analog speeds may be more conducive to deep thought and creative problem-solving.

The psychologist Daniel Kahneman has written extensively about the benefits of slowing our thought processes in order to access not just our intuitive and automatic conclusions, but our more reflective reasoning capacities. The more we understand about the brain, the more we realize that a slower pace can be beneficial.

For example, we're often told to "take a deep breath" in order to calm down, but slowing your breathing doesn't just relax your muscles—it can also have an effect on your brain. Coherent breathing is a method that trains people to slow respiration down to six breaths (or fewer) per minute. It turns out that slower breathing can improve your attention span, your decision making, and your cognitive function.

But the speed of our devices quickly began to change our understanding of time in the nondigital world. How long do you wait after sending a text, for example, before you become impatient for a response? How about an email? Business communication sped up exponentially, and while that brought many benefits, it also altered our social expectations. Researchers at USC analyzed 16 billion emails and found that once you've hit send, you're likely to get a response within two minutes, and most people reply in less than an hour.

Let's say you work for a shoe manufacturer. Is it possible that the same shipping receipt that reached you over the course of hours or days in 2001 will now cause a major catastrophe if it's not received and responded to within minutes? Has our business truly become more urgent, or is it only expectations that have changed?

Your manager may get annoyed when you don't answer an email immediately, but I'm not convinced immediate answers are best for business. Perhaps time to reflect before answering will improve the quality of the response.

I've tested this myself, by purposely waiting for days to respond to texts and emails. Nothing exploded. I didn't lose any clients. All of my work got done, and the delay didn't cause any issues, serious or otherwise. Since then, I've continued the practice by checking my email only a few times a day. Once people realized I might not respond to them immediately, they stopped expecting an immediate response and I stopped sending emails, for the most part, at nine p.m.

The pace is even faster for texts. Ninety-five percent of them are read within three minutes, and it takes about 90 seconds to get a response. Ninety seconds! That means we often stop what we're doing—getting dressed, eating dinner, talking to someone in front of you—in order to respond to "How's it going?" Psychologist Adam Alter noted in his popular TED Talk that the smartphone is "where your humanity lives. And right now, it's in a very small box."

Tech is the cause of many disruptions in our lives. For one thing, it interferes with our sleep. Most of us sleep with our phones in our hands or right beside us, and a third of us admit to checking our phones at some point in the middle of the night. Now, you may think it's no big deal to take a glance at your phone when you get up to use the bathroom, or to take it with you, but your brain might disagree.

The light emitted by phones and tablets fools our brains into thinking it's daytime, for one thing. Most electronics use blue light that has a short wavelength and is highly visible but very energy efficient. Blue light is great during daylight hours. It's environmentally friendly and it can boost your mood and your energy.

The problem is, blue light can cause damage to your eyes over the long term, and it can suppress the release of melatonin, the hormone that helps you fall asleep and stay asleep. When scientists at Harvard tested the effects of blue light versus green light, they found the blue suppressed melatonin production and disrupted circadian rhythms (which govern sleep and waking times) for about twice as long as green. The message here is that if you're looking at your device within two to three hours before bedtime, you could be screwing up your sleep cycle. Millions of years of evolution have trained our bodies to react to the rise and fall of the sun, and adapting away from that will not be a rapid process.

Further, the phone is very stimulating, both cognitively and visually. Many apps are meant to engage your mind, and they're quite good at it. An alert mind, though, is not a mind that's ready to rest. On top of all this, your brain doesn't really distinguish between posting on Facebook and working in the office. If you're prone to using social media or answering texts and emails while you're in bed, you're telling your brain that the bed is a place for work, not rest.

The harmful effects trickle out beyond the bedroom, though. The truth is, when smartphones are overused, they have a strong impact on the brain that's mostly negative. Your mind treats all those notifications that come in as seriously as it treats a fire alarm or a knock on the door. Basically, whenever you have your phone at hand, your brain is spending a certain amount of energy preparing to respond to possible emergencies.

A little chime sounds, indicating that you've gotten a text message, and it activates the stress hormones in your head. Your body goes into fight-or-flight mode and your muscles may even contract, preparing you to run. Now imagine that process being repeated hundreds of times, perhaps thousands, over the course of a day, every time your phone vibrates or makes noise. The effect can be so strong that you may feel sore after your muscles spent the day contracting and releasing.

Turns out, the more interaction you have with your phone, the "noisier" your brain is. The noise I'm referring to here is called "neuronal variability." It's a term that describes a certain kind of extraneous, possibly distracting, electrical activity inside our skulls. It's static interfering with our brain's radio signals.

So our phones interfere with sleep and focus and stress, and there's also the not insignificant cost we pay for checking texts while we're on a conference call or answering emails while reading a book. This is a good opportunity to revisit the issue of multitasking and the price we pay for trying to do it.

It takes time for our brains to break away from one task and focus in on a new one, and some psychologists say about 40 percent of our cognitive effort is devoted to switching back and forth between texts and emails and social media and website links.

While we're working on one thing, our prefrontal cortex (just behind the forehead, where executive decisions are made) brings both halves of the brain to bear on the task at hand. When we try to multitask (and that's what is happening when we answer emails while working on a report), the brain splits the two sides into two separate teams. Our attention is almost literally divided. We forget things more easily and are three times more likely to make a mistake.

The indisputable truth is, our phones are deeply distracting to our brains. The mere presence of a smartphone is so agitating to our gray matter that it interferes with our ability to perform basic cognitive tasks.

To give you an example of how this plays out in real time, let me tell you about my writing process before and during my cross-country train trip. Just before embarking, I wrote several blog posts about train travel and my decision to spend two weeks on Amtrak. It took me about four hours to finish them on average, as I sat at my computer at home.

On the train, I blogged every day, but I often didn't have a Wi-Fi signal and therefore could not flip to other browser tabs or check my email while working. I finished those posts in about forty minutes. Even though multitasking makes me feel productive, I actually saved nearly three and a half hours by focusing on my writing and nothing else.

I told you the list of damage caused by tech would be fairly long, but we're nearly through it. Here's an interesting wrinkle: Access to the internet also makes us think we know more than we do. This one is important because it directly supports the idea that tech doesn't always make us more efficient but instead creates an illusion of efficiency.

Researchers at Yale conducted a series of experiments involving more than a thousand people. In one study, participants were told how zippers work. Half of them were instructed to confirm the details of the explanation by searching online. Then they were all asked a bunch of totally unrelated questions like "How do tornadoes form?" Those who'd been allowed to look online for information about zippers were more likely to think they knew more about *everything* they were asked, even weather, history, and food.

Studies show that online research doesn't make us much more knowledgeable, but it significantly increases our confidence in our knowledge. Looking up your symptoms online, for example, is overwhelmingly likely to provide you with an incorrect diagnosis. And yet people who use virtual symptom checkers are more likely to doubt their doctor's advice and search for alternative remedies.

We've seen the same results in the financial world, where online research on any topic makes you more confident in your overall knowledge and more likely to bet on what you think you know by investing based more on self-assurance than on actual data.

Perhaps the most damning piece of evidence in the debate over technology is the large number of tech workers who restrict their kids from using smartphones and tablets. Athena Chavarria of Facebook told the *New York Times,* "I am convinced the Devil lives in our phones and is wreaking havoc on our children."

Steve Jobs famously did not allow his own kids to use iPads, saying that he and his wife limited the technology their kids used at home. One of the founders of Twitter, Evan Williams, gave his kids actual books instead of tablets, and Chris Anderson, former editor of *Wired,* has said he severely limits screen time in his home because he is painfully aware of the damage tech can do. "I've seen it in myself," he said. "I don't want to see that happen to my kids."

Tech workers and software developers are partly responsible for the addictive nature of our devices, so it's no wonder they're concerned about the impact that tech has on their families. This should give us all pause when we consider how much we use smartphones and tablets. Would you eat a meal that the chef wouldn't serve to his own family?

Let's get to the last item on our list, and this one's a doozy. Digital devices are having a massive effect on our social interaction. This is, to me, the most troubling and dangerous side effect of smartphone addiction.

The initial intent behind texting and social media was good. People honestly believed tech would bring us closer by making communication quicker and cheaper. It has accomplished the latter two but not the first. In fact, tech has increased our isolation. The danger is, of course, that much like our increased knowledge after online searches, tech gives us an illusion of effective communication. It makes us think we're connecting in a substantial way, so we miss the warning signs.

Having hundreds of "friends" on Facebook or followers on Twitter is not the same as having true friendships with real people. I can't say it any more plainly than that. More and more, we are investing in horizontal relationships (widespread and superficial) rather than vertical (focused and in-depth), and we may simply be overwhelmed by superficial connections.

Up until the twentieth century, humans dealt with just a few dozen people over the course of their lives. We are healthiest when we have a small number of confidants, a slightly larger number of good friends, a larger number of acquaintances, and so on, not dozens and dozens of "friends" online and almost no intimate friendships. In 1985, Americans reported having three close confidants. By 2004, it was down to two, and about one in four say they don't have anyone at all they can talk to about personal issues.

I truly believe that some of the harmful effects of social media are caused by overload. We are daily (sometimes hourly) bombarded with emotional pleas for attention and interaction. One of the more common types of messages on Facebook goes something like this: "I'm conducting a test to see if anyone actually reads my posts. If you read this, please tell me how we met." If you can't remember how you met that person and don't usually read their posts, seeing that kind of message can make you feel guilty. It's perfectly natural to want to retreat from human contact in the face of overwhelming emotional stimuli.

Through an understanding of my evolutionary imperatives, I am able to better understand why social media exhausts me. I enjoy it, but it stresses me out, and that's partly because I simply can't keep track of everyone's marriages and parents and careers. I want to care, but it's really difficult.

As the anthropologist and evolutionary psychologist Robin Dunbar said, "Our minds are not designed to allow us to have more than a limited number of people in our social world. The emotional and psychological investments that a close relationship requires are considerable, and the emotional capital we have available is limited."

His research led to the creation of the "Dunbar number": the number of relationships that a human being can reasonably maintain. The Dunbar number is 150. By the end of 2018, I had more than 8,000 "friends" on Facebook and more than 16,000 followers on Twitter, all of whom sent me messages and commented on my photos. Many know my dog's name and my favorite foods and what I do with my time. It's simply too much. The internet is perhaps *too* efficient at connecting people.

I was struck by a string of tweets sent by the author Joe Hill in 2018. He wrote: "The promise of social media is that it would connect people, but I think eleven years in, to me anyway, it's clear it's actually much better at dividing us and making us feel sad. . . . I have made some great friends here and had some good—some amazing—conversations. But I've gradually become convinced that the net effect of social media isn't much good for me."

Hill eventually returned to Twitter and is still active on the platform. I can hardly fault him for that. Platforms like Twitter and WhatsApp have some incredible advantages. The problem with them, just as with our smartphones and tablets, is not use but *overuse.* Issues arise when we try to replace what already works with tech that cannot compare with the real thing.

I asked the social psychologist Juliana Schroeder about this and she said, "We're trying to make the text-based medium a better way to convey thought. But these text-based tools are really blunt and less effective. Speech is so much more sophisticated. It's been around so much longer than writing."

I asked if at some point text might become as effective as talking, and she said it might be possible *in five to ten thousand years.* So by the year 7020, text may have evolved to be as comprehensive a communication tool as the human voice.

With all the evidence that surrounds us, it might seem reasonable to assume smartphones are the villain in this story, but I don't think we can blame tech for what's going wrong. Our devices are wonderful, but we misuse them. Social media is a perfect example. Research has shown that when used properly and proactively, social media can make you happier.

In practice, that's not what happens, of course: Social media makes most people miserable. We know that most people "lurk" on Facebook, for example. They read other people's posts and glance through their pictures during most of their time spent on the platform, ostensibly comparing their own lives to someone else's curated experience. That behavior erodes well-being and eventually makes you unhappy. As it turns out, less than 10 percent of our activity on Facebook involves actively communicating with someone else.

Social media is good for us when we're using it proactively and intentionally, not while we're staring at other people's content. So instead of helping us, social media is wasting our time and making us sad. In fact, one survey showed more people want to quit social media than to stop smoking. I imagine that's a pretty good indicator that we're addicted and that we recognize this addiction is not good for us.

I'm not shaming anyone for their social media use, by the way. It's affirming to tweet something out and see that hundreds of people have liked what you said. It's exciting to feel that you're "chatting" back and forth with someone who thinks like you do. Even the insults (when they're not too abusive or threatening) can be pleasurable if lots of people leap to your defense.

Even after all my research, it took me two years to finally delete my Facebook account. I installed an extension on my web browser to limit the time I spent on Twitter, and then found myself cheating by using a different browser when I'd used up all of my tweeting time. I found I couldn't just decide to stop playing games on my phone; I had to delete the apps completely.

It's becoming increasingly clear in recent years that we're not wholly to blame for our digital addiction. The former Google design ethicist Tristan Harris writes often and eloquently about the ways tech "hijacks our psychological vulnerabilities." Among other things, many designers follow the slot machine model of driving interaction with apps. They create a system of variable rewards in which you sometimes get a reward for pulling the lever (refreshing your inbox or Twitter feed) and sometimes get nothing.

"When we pull our phones out of our pocket, we're *playing a slot machine* to see what notifications we got," Harris writes. "When we swipe down our finger to scroll the Instagram feed, we're *playing a slot machine* to see what photo comes next." Experts have shown that people become addicted to slot machines three to four times faster than to other types of gambling, partly because of the uncertainty involved. It's no wonder software designers would emulate that model.

Gabe Zichermann, a gamification expert, told *Time* magazine that many companies were trying to create a "diaper product." Zichermann explained that the underlying concept is to "make something so addictive, [the users] don't even want to get up to pee." Or sleep, apparently, since the CEO of Netflix, Reed Hastings, told investors that the company's real competition is sleep.

Boy, does it work. Netflix eliminated the closing and opening titles for many shows so another episode starts before you've even registered that the previous one ended. I generally go to bed at ten p.m. but binged the entire season of *The Great British Baking Show* one night and was shocked to see, when I blearily peered at the clock, that it was 2:15 in the morning. The show was the equivalent of a bucket of popcorn at the movies: I just kept mindlessly eating until the entire bucket was empty.

The addiction to tech is also driven by FOMO: the fear of missing out. FOMO combines widespread social anxiety with inherent human competitiveness and an existing addiction to social media. The final cocktail is a heady mix.

Many social media platforms encourage constant updates and unending discussion or commentary. If you let a few hours pass before checking back in with Twitter, you may not understand the jokes and sarcastic comments in your feed because you missed an initial viral tweet. This feeds an all-too-common fear of being an outsider. It drives us back to refresh that feed over and over again.

By exploiting this fear, software designers are actually tapping in to an ancient survival mechanism. In centuries past, our ability to remain alert to potential threats was often the difference between life and death. The urge to have the most current information is primal. As the clinical psychologist Anita Sanz wrote on Quora, there is a region in the brain that's responsible for warning us when we're not getting all the information we need or are being excluded from our community.

"That specialized part of the brain," she writes, "is a part of the limbic system, the amygdala, whose job it is to detect whether something could be a threat to our survival. Not having vital information or getting the impression that one is not a part of the 'in' group is enough for many individuals' amygdalas to engage the stress or activation response or the 'fight or flight' response."

That's a powerful force encouraging us to return to our Facebook feed every twenty minutes or so, because a primal urge makes us believe it's an efficient way to stay informed and, therefore, safe. The amygdala prioritizes our Twitter feed out of fear. Subconsciously, we think staying current on social media is our best option: more efficient and more secure.

As I alluded to earlier, though, taking in information rapidly is not conducive to reflection or reasoning. When we're skimming through tiny tidbits of news while scanning social media, we're only able to access our automatic and instinctive thought processes. We are thinking in knee jerks and so make rational errors. We don't question assumptions or spot logical fallacies. All too often, we take in misinformation and then spread it.

As I struggle with my own addiction and come to terms with how tech has interfered with my personal relationships, it's reassuring to find that many of my friends are going through the same thing. If the expectations of our peers are driving at least some of our addictions, perhaps we can decide together to change those expectations.

The research is quite clear on this. The single most highly engineered productivity tool of the past two decades is negatively affecting the quality of our lives. This is a global problem, raising concerns from India to the Netherlands to Brazil and China.

It's clear, in light of my struggles and those of many others, that this is not just an issue for young people. The technical term for smartphone addiction is *nomophobia,* or the fear of being without your phone. Even senior citizens are prone to it. Software designers have been so successful at drawing our attention that 10 percent of people admit to checking their phones during sex and 12 percent say they've looked at their phones while in the shower. (Let's hope they had waterproof devices.)

As our use of social media and tech has risen, so has loneliness, social isolation, and suicide.

But none of this—the addictive apps and the fear of missing out—would be quite as successful were it not for the existing emphasis on productivity and efficiency that started dominating lives in the nineteenth century. A person who can leave their cell phone at home is not an important person, right? Kids see their parents answering emails at the dinner table and make assumptions about the relative importance of the meal versus the email. "Many young adults turn to the screen because they feel it's the only authorized recreation in a culture of constant work," says Rachel Simmons of Smith College.

That culture of constant work existed before Nokia released the first smartphone. It existed before Microsoft Windows or the iMac. When you're looking for something to blame for our current state of stress and anxiety and social isolation, you can start with tech, but you have to end in the workplace. The office is where the dysfunction began, not the internet.

Tech is a tool that should be used for specific tasks and then set aside. If you use social media to stay in touch with friends and family, check in once a day and then get back to real life. At the moment, our machines have imprisoned us, but we have the power to free ourselves and shrug off the yoke.

Even if we did that now—asserted control over our devices and limited our use of social media—the underlying issues would not go away, just as disconnecting from my devices didn't ultimately make me less anxious or allay my feelings of overwork. That's why tech is not the problem. It's a symptom.

Although we can't draw a direct line from the rise of smartphones and social media to the increase in social isolation, there is definitely a correlation. According to a survey from Cigna, the most isolated and loneliest among us are the most technologically savvy: young people born since the mid-1990s.

It's important to note the distinction between loneliness and being alone, by the way. People who interact regularly with others, who converse with coworkers and text their friends, may appear to have a fulfilling social life but may be secretly suffering the effects of social isolation.

This issue is one in which perception truly is reality. Perceived isolation is loneliness, and the number of people who say they have no close friends is on the rise.

Loneliness is caused by a lack of intimate contacts, contacts that are rarely found online. Facebook may dramatically increase the number of social interactions you have over the course of a day but decrease the number of significant connections. Among all our memes about how much we love canceling plans and our proclivity for rejecting phone calls in favor of texts is a sad statement about twenty-first-century life.

Having hundreds of friends on Facebook or lots of Twitter followers doesn't fill the hole inside. Digital interaction is simply not the same as talking to someone or spending time with a real person, in the flesh. When you are visually acknowledged with a wave or a smile, it creates feelings of social connectedness that generally don't arise from a "like" on Instagram.

What's true of digital connections is also true of the office. Relationships with coworkers also do not satisfy the need for intimate interaction. Those friendships are often dependent on the job, meaning that your employer has ultimate control.

Your interactions take place at the workplace and are often about the workplace. If you're laid off, you probably won't see that person again. It's rare that a work relationship gives you the same stability and acceptance as a connection you might make with someone who will still talk to you even when you take a new job.

Among the many changes wrought by our increasing focus on work, productivity, and efficiency, the loss of friendships that develop over time and are, by definition, inefficient is probably the most damaging. Workplaces are not families, and coworkers are often not intimate friends. Talking with a Twitter friend 140 characters at a time is incredibly efficient but ultimately of little emotional value. In order to have the kinds of relationships we need, we'll have to start redrawing the boundary lines between office and home.

We know the problem; now it's time to talk about solutions.

PART II

Leaving the Cult— How to Go from Life Hack to Life Back

Life-Back One

CHALLENGE YOUR PERCEPTIONS

> You'd think people, just out of self-interest, would realize what's good for them and come around.
>
> —
>
> ROY BAUMEISTER

IT WAS SELF-INTEREST THAT led me to this field of study. I had reached a stage of my life where I could not continue doing what I was doing. I was anxious and irritable and perpetually exhausted. That's not what I wanted my life to look like, and a vastly increased income had made it all worse, not better.

I was doing what I was told would make my life better: finding strategies to streamline my chores, using productivity journals, following a guaranteed exercise regime, and working very, very hard. I became more successful in my career, but that success was not accompanied by less stress and increased well-being. Instead, the more success I had, the more anxious I became.

I had spent years peeling back the layers to find out what had gone wrong. The next step was to devise a solution. Luckily, that wasn't difficult once I learned how humans lived before James Watt first decided to tinker with a steam engine.

The revelation that emerged after all my research into neuroscience and evolutionary biology and primatology was that we know how to do this already. We've gotten a little off-track, but we can right the ship now.

As soon as the business community landed on efficiency as a pathway to greater profits, many other considerations were made a lower priority, and the same has occurred in our personal lives. As we have become more efficient, we have also become more fragile. Consider the difference between the goal of efficiency—adaptation to an existing environment—and the goal of resilience—the ability to adapt to changes in one's environment.

"Resilient systems," writes Roger Martin in the *Harvard Business Review,* "are typically characterized by the very features—diversity and redundancy, or slack—that efficiency seeks to destroy." Essentially, we adapted to the environment that seemed ideal two hundred years ago, using systems that worked well in business when manufacturing powered our economies and millions of people worked in factories.

As our environment changed, we failed to adapt and instead doubled down on the strategy that seemed to work in 1880, although I would argue that it wasn't particularly good for the majority of human beings at any point in history.

Now we've reached a precipice. The dark cloud that has loomed on the horizon for two centuries is now above our heads. It's time to change.

What I thought was a personal problem is in fact more widespread. Many of my friends are experiencing the same frustration and anxiety, and so are their coworkers and their families. I am merely a reflection of the culture in which I was raised, as are we all.

Before we take any action, perhaps it's best to be still for just a moment so we can look around and take stock. It's important to have a clear (and honest) picture of where we stand. It's possible we're not truly aware of our own habits and behavior. Many people in the industrialized world have what I call "busyness delusion," or the mistaken belief that we are busier than we really are. This may be difficult to accept, but many of us tend to think we work more hours than we actually do.

I understand if you are immediately put off by that sentence. I know I regularly feel exhausted at the end of my day and I'm barely able to drag myself on a walk with my dog, let alone start cooking a meal. Perhaps that's why the meal kit industry, which began in 2007, grew so quickly that eleven years later, it was worth up to $5 billion. If you immediately thought, *I really am working too many hours. It's not in my head,* I understand. I thought the same thing. Bear with me.

Since the mid-1960s we have conducted time-use surveys in the United States and therefore have a pretty accurate understanding of average work schedules. Men today work about twelve hours *less* per week than they did in the 1970s. Women work more, partly because many more women have full-time jobs than they did fifty years ago, but their unpaid labor has dropped by double digits.

When working mothers kept diaries for several weeks recently, they found they had much more time with their children than they thought. In fact, the total time spent working has not risen since the 1990s and parents in general are spending more hours with their children every week.

Still, many of us feel we are working too many hours and are constantly pressed for time. That's why it's crucial to determine just how your hours are being spent, so you can identify the source of your fatigue. A useful tool in this circumstance is a simple diary of some kind. If you keep track of your schedule in a detailed way for a couple weeks, you'll be able to get a clear picture of how your time is spent. Before you address any of the other issues associated with addiction to efficiency and productivity, you must have an accurate assessment of how that addiction is influencing your habits and choices.

Regardless of whether you're really working excessive hours or not, *believing* that you are short on time has real, damaging effects. Keeping your eye on the clock, even subconsciously, can lead to a sharp drop in performance. Research shows that when you are highly aware of time passing, it even makes you less compassionate toward others. What's more, it can interfere with your ability to make rational decisions.

Because of that, feeling pressed for time can lead you to make bad choices about how to use your time. This can quickly become a vicious cycle. Having no clear understanding of how you spend your time can leave you feeling more overwhelmed than necessary, which can cause you to make decisions that lead to more stress and anxiety, which feeds the sense that you're pressed for time, and you end up feeling more overwhelmed than necessary.

An understanding of how our hours are spent is known as "time perception." People who have little time perception spend more time watching TV or lingering on social media sites, and they often report feeling overwhelmed.

On the other hand, people who have high time perception scores, who are very aware of their schedules, actually tend to set aside more time for leisure. These people allow for time to contemplate and reflect, and that gives them the sense that they have more time. This is not a vicious cycle, but a virtuous one. You may believe you can relax if you put in a few more hours and get ahead of your workload, but actually you're more likely to reduce your stress level by taking a break.

Increasing my time perception has made a radical difference in my life. At the end of the day, I feel accomplished because I'm fully aware of all that I've done, but I also feel relaxed because I know I spent a couple hours sitting on my porch reading magazines.

This one small change—becoming more aware of what you do between waking and sleeping—could have a cascade of benefits. As I mentioned, it may leave you with a sense that you have more time to take care of both your needs and your desires and, as it turns out, that feeling is better for you than a raise in pay. A study in 2009 showed that even after controlling for income, if you make someone believe they have time to spare, they feel healthier and happier.

You'll notice I said "make someone believe they have free time." That describes a feeling, not necessarily a tangible reality. No one in the experiment actually found more free time; participants just *felt* they had more. And that feeling can come from keeping track of your hours, without changing a thing! That happens not by knuckling down and working more, but by taking more breaks. Counterintuitive, but perfectly true.

Obviously, there are basic needs that must be met. Some people have to work several jobs in order to keep a roof over their heads and food on the table. It has not been long since I was in that situation, and I would have laughed at someone who told me either to lean in to my work or lean out. I was in fight-or-flight mode. For some, of course, a sense of time affluence may be out of reach.

However, if you are not scrambling to pay for water, food, clothing, and shelter, you might discover that increasing your time perception (becoming aware of how you spend your time) will bring greater happiness than a higher salary. And in any case, once you venture into the upper-income brackets, higher pay is often associated with a lower sense of well-being and less enjoyment at work. That is one of the ironies of our current system: Pursuing higher salaries can bring less happiness, not more.

We work long hours in order to make more money, not realizing that once we've met our fundamental needs, it is leisure time that increases happiness, not necessarily extra cash. If you have time to relax and you're not using it, that's a serious issue. It may be you're experiencing unnecessary stress if you think there aren't enough hours in the day and *you're wrong*.

Track Your Time

Begin by keeping a diary and tracking your activities. Be honest! If you spent a half hour on Twitter, note that down. If you discover that you spent twenty minutes looking at shoes online, write that down too. After all, no one will see this diary but you, and the more honest you are, the more helpful this exercise will be.

Once you have a clear idea of how much you're working, how many hours are devoted to social media, and how much time you spend on leisure, you can begin to ask yourself some important questions. For example, *How much time do I want to spend on social media or email? Do I want to exercise every day? How much time should it take to eat dinner?* Use the answers to these questions to create guidelines for yourself.

I spent three weeks keeping a diary of my time in order to get a clear picture of my habits. To do this, I simply bought a notebook and divided my day into half-hour chunks. Every few hours, I would write down what I'd been doing. At the end of three weeks, I realized that I spent about two and a half hours on email every day, and a couple more hours reading Facebook posts and tweets. Weekly, I spent more than three hours idly shopping on the internet.

I'm only awake for about sixteen hours, so it was a shock to discover that more than a third of my day was spent doing mostly useless things online. Instead of reading a book while I sat in waiting rooms or on the train, I would refresh my Instagram feed and "like" my friends' posts. That's not how I wanted to spend my day, and, frankly, I'd had no idea that's what I was doing with my time.

Make a Schedule

I decided that I wanted to spend no more than ninety minutes a day on email and social media. (Since then, I've pared that down to an hour.) In order to accomplish that, I knew I'd have to make drastic changes in my habits. So I created two ideal schedules, one for gym days and one for the rest. I work from home when I'm not traveling, so weekends don't have the same significance to me. You might find it more useful to create a schedule for weekdays and another for weekends.

I asked myself, *What's the ideal use of my time on a daily basis?* I created a list of the things I wanted to do every day, plus the things I had to do, then spread them over my sixteen waking hours. Here's what those schedules look like:

Gym Days

7:00—wake/take care of the dog/dress
7:30—walk the dog
8:30—gym
9:30—shower
9:45—meditate
10:00—email and social media
10:30—write/work
12:30—lunch
1:00—short walk
1:30—write/work
3:30—free time and meditate
5:30—walk the dog
6:30—dinner
7:30—free time
9:00—bath or self-care
10:00—bed

Non-Gym Days

7:00—wake/take care of the dog/dress
7:30—walk the dog
8:00—meditate
8:30—house chores and errands
9:30—email and social media
10:00—write
12:30—lunch
1:00—short walk
1:30—write
3:30—free time and meditate
5:30—walk the dog
6:30—dinner
7:30—free time
9:00—bath or self-care
10:00—bed

These schedules are *very* flexible. Often, I have to do interviews or meet with friends, and that means my day changes. There's no point in agonizing over whether I've stuck to the timeline or not because I don't see these schedules as restrictive but supportive. They are merely suggestions. If I spend forty minutes on social media some days instead of thirty, I don't sweat it, and my dog doesn't always get three walks a day. (Sometimes she gets four.)

Obviously, if I'm traveling, these schedules change quite a bit. And yet I've found that the basic underpinnings remain the same. I nearly always find time for the activities listed here, even if they occur at very different times. This is an ideal schedule, remember, and ideal is rarely the same as real.

Since creating these schedules, I check email once an hour and generally limit my social media time to one hour a day. Sometimes a couple hours go by before I realize that I haven't looked at my inbox, which was unheard of in past years. On weekends, I often forget about email completely after I check it in the morning. I can't even describe how liberating that is, and how relaxing. I installed an app on my phone that limits my access when it's turned on. If I start the app and then try to unlock my phone, it says "Really??" and I quickly put it down.

I printed my schedules and hung copies in my office. After following them for a few weeks, I was surprised to discover that I had plenty of time to do everything I wanted to do, with hours to spare. It was a powerful moment for me. When I truly understood that my work was *not* out of control or unmanageable, a tangible wave of relief swept through my body. I had enough time!

Life-Back Two

TAKE THE MEDIA OUT OF YOUR SOCIAL

> A true friend is the greatest of all blessings, and that which we take the least care of all to acquire.
>
> —FRANÇOIS DE LA ROCHEFOUCAULD

THE EUPHORIA I FELT after gaining control of my schedule was, sadly, short-lived. I had dinner with a couple friends just days after completing that exercise and almost immediately, everyone began talking about how busy they were. It may have been the first thing they talked about. I said hello, it's so good to see you, how are you, and the answer was, "Crazy busy. You can't even imagine." That comment was followed by a description of all the things going on in each person's life.

I knew better, and yet I found myself joining in, reciting a laundry list of my projects and appointments and responsibilities. I was literally in the middle of saying that I didn't have enough time to schedule a dentist appointment when I realized

I was lying. I had just proven to myself that I had enough time, so why was I talking about how busy I was?

The answer is, of course, peer pressure. I wanted to prove I was as important as my friends were. I wanted to demonstrate that I was in demand and I wanted to be part of the group. So I fell into some old habits. That's why the next step to breaking the efficiency addiction is to stop comparing yourself to the other people in your life.

Stop Making Comparisons

It's a common mistake to evaluate ourselves and our lives by comparison instead of through objective measures. In other words, we strive to be as busy as or busier than our friends and colleagues instead of deciding what's best for us.

This is problematic because most people are not entirely truthful when they tell others about their habits and their workload. Data from the Labor Department shows Americans tend to overstate their working hours by up to 10 percent, and the more hours they claim to work, the less accurate their estimate is. People who said they worked seventy-five hours a week actually put in fifty hours, for example.

That means you can't win the comparison game, as people will continue to up the ante. If you constantly compare yourself to what others say about themselves, you may always feel lazy by comparison. (If it makes you feel any better, you're probably overstating your own workload when you talk to other people.)

There's another interesting wrinkle here: Because we have cut back on our in-person interactions with neighbors and friends, the people we compare ourselves to are often not the people who lead similar lives to our own. This adds another layer to the inaccuracy of our judgments.

Imagine a barbecue in your backyard in 1970. Your neighbors come over and talk about their new TV or dishwasher, maybe brag about their new Pontiac Firebird. In decades past, "keeping up with the Joneses" meant maintaining a standard of living that was comparable to your immediate community. That community was mostly made up of people who were making about the same salary you were and enjoying a relatively similar standard of living.

Since we have quit having those barbecues and stopped attending Rotary Club meetings, we don't compare ourselves to our neighbors and colleagues anymore. Instead, we measure ourselves against the Real Housewives of whatever city and the other people we see on TV or Instagram. As the sociologist Juliet Schor explains, we are now trying to keep up not with the Joneses but with the Kardashians.

People used to yearn to break into the economic class just above their own. Now we strive to emulate the top 20 percent of income earners, because those are the families we're watching on TV. Those are the photos we see online and the videos that pop up in our Facebook feeds. Many people around the world are now more knowledgeable about the daily lives of reality TV stars or celebrities than about the lives of other people who live on their block. The more TV you watch, it turns out, the more likely you are to overestimate how much other people make and how many things they own.

At this point, Americans don't think someone is wealthy unless their income is about $2.5 million a year. That's thirty times the actual amount an individual needs in order to be classified as upper income in the United States, and thirty times the average net worth of American households.

Comparing ourselves to the highest earners in the country has made us all feel poor and might be driving us to work harder and put in more hours in a futile attempt to create the lifestyle we think others have. Scientists have repeatedly shown that people who are asked to compare their lives to the lives of others immediately think of celebrities, CEOs, and political leaders. Celebrities' lifestyles are publicized and so we see them constantly. They have become our benchmark. I don't need to mention that for all but a very few of us, that benchmark is unattainable. So the comparisons we draw are making us feel like failures.

To be fair, the human compulsion to compare ourselves to others is deeply ingrained and not unhelpful. It's a by-product of our evolutionary need to fit into a group, to make sure we are not outsiders.

If you're afraid to climb a steep hill but your friends are already clambering up the rocky slope, comparing your fear to their bravery might motivate you to climb. If your coworkers all jog during their lunch break, you might join them. If you live with someone who eats a balanced diet, measuring your own food choices with theirs might have a positive influence. However, these are all comparisons made using real evidence and tangible information about people you are seeing face-to-face. These are comparisons based on what members of your own community are really doing, not based on what distant others *seem* to be doing.

So the urge to make comparisons is not necessarily bad unless our perception of others is inaccurate and therefore the comparisons aren't valid. One modern danger is that social media skews our view of others' lives, and that makes any comparison problematic. Most people believe their friends' social lives are richer and more interesting than they actually are. This was demonstrated in a 2017 study published in the *Journal of Personality and Social Psychology*.

Researchers discovered that many people imagine their peers hang out with friends on a regular basis. They think their friends are going to parties and generally being quite social, while they spend most nights at home. The actual data, though, suggest our peers are not as social as we believe they are.

We've heard often that what we see on Twitter or Snapchat is a curated, heavily edited version of our friends' lives. It's not real because it's not complete. Yet subconsciously, we are still using that inaccurate picture as a basis for comparison.

When we compare ourselves to the imagined social lives of our friends and coworkers, we believe we are more socially isolated than average. This depresses our sense of well-being and makes us feel that we don't belong. As the report from that 2017 study says, "Social comparisons can be associated with feelings of inferiority, envy, anxiety, and depression."

All in all, this results in the creation of two types of unattainable ideals: one based on the lives of celebrities and public figures, the other based on distorted reality, incorrect assumptions, and misperceptions about the people we know. Striving to live up to these impossible ideals has led to a widespread crisis of perfectionism, especially among young people.

Research shows that perfectionism has been increasing among college students since the 1980s. An emphasis on competitive individualism has driven this, especially in the United States, United Kingdom, and Canada. Now, twenty-somethings are more demanding of themselves than ever and more demanding of others. They expect perfection and are far less forgiving of mistakes than previous generations.

Students will delete social media posts that don't get at least one like per minute. Jared Yates Sexton of Georgia Southern University says that when his students are writing essays, they are "obsessed with creating a perfect artifact." He and other teachers have started using a process called the "Shitty First Draft."

The concept was popularized by the author Anne Lamott in her book *Bird by Bird.* She wrote: "The first draft is the child's draft, where you let it all pour out and then let it romp all over the place knowing that no one is going to see it and that you can shape it later." Sexton says he sometimes struggles to get his students to write anything, so paralyzed are they by the pressure to make their work flawless. "So many of them are looking to write the perfect essay," he says, "they spend more time with anxiety than they do producing."

This perfectionism is a by-product of a society that is outwardly focused and constantly making comparisons. You might feel good about the dinner you make until you look on Instagram, or you may love a certain TV show until you see it being dragged by people on Twitter who claim that only an idiot would enjoy that show. Rachel Simmons, author of *Odd Girl Out: The Hidden Culture of Aggression in Girls,* tells me that perfectionism has risen because "the home has been turned into part of the market."

Social media sites like Pinterest provide a constant stream of images that convince us we could and should be doing better. "Pinterest," Simmons says, "now makes people think their bedsheets aren't as good as they thought they were and your cupcakes are hideous compared to everyone else's." If we're sitting at home and discover we have some downtime, Simmons explains, we think, *Maybe I'll make some new curtains.*

It is the comparison that makes us feel less than, especially comparisons made at a distance. I'm not surprised, and neither is Simmons, that teenagers are now feeling more pressure than ever to be perfect. While not surprising, this rising tide of perfectionism is extremely dangerous.

This self-inflicted pressure has a very high cost on the human mind and body. Unreasonably high standards and severe self-criticism are linked to high blood pressure, depression, eating disorders, and suicidal ideation. Therapists will tell you that you cannot both strive to be perfect and enjoy good mental health. They are mutually exclusive.

While correlation is not causation, it's important to note that suicides among young people have risen by 56 percent since 1999. One Pennsylvania teacher connects the rise in suicides to the increase in standardized testing. "American students are increasingly being sorted and evaluated by reference to their test score rather than their classroom grade or other academic indicators," Steven Singer wrote on *HuffPost.* "Students are no longer 6th, 7th or 8th graders. They're Below Basics, Basics, Proficients and Advanced. The classes they're placed in, the style of teaching, even personal rewards and punishments are determined by a single score."

Keep in mind that standardized testing was conceived as a highly efficient method for tracking student progress and holding schools accountable. Standardized testing is an institutionalized system for comparison, to determine what is average and what is outside "normal" parameters.

The rise in perfectionism seems to have begun about forty years ago, which means that many of those early high achievers are parents now and are unknowingly passing that perfectionism along to their children. "They can feel our anxiety about them," Rachel Simmons tells me. "They can feel our dissatisfaction with who they are. Why doesn't my kid want to build things? Why doesn't my daughter have many friends? They only realize they're not okay when we send those messages to them." Parents may think they're helping their kids succeed by pushing them to reach the top of the class and be the best at whatever they do, but they may actually be increasing the pressure to win or go home.

I asked Simmons how bad the perfectionism problem is and she answered, "I vaguely hate myself as a parent and I'm a parenting expert. So what does that tell you?" Parents are particularly susceptible to the fear that they're not doing enough. That's not a new phenomenon, but the measure of what's "enough" has moved significantly higher than in previous decades.

This is the danger of unhealthy comparisons. When we measure ourselves against unrealistic or distorted ideals, we can do real psychological damage in trying to match them. I'm reminded of the story of Sisyphus, always trying to roll a boulder up a hill, never getting it to the top, never allowed to rest. How much worse would it have been for him if he'd thought he was the only one of his friends who couldn't get that damn rock all the way up the hill?

We can end this toxic habit of constant comparison. Stop checking the internet to look at how other people are doing things, for one. If you want to make cupcakes, grab a recipe and make them. Don't scour Pinterest for the "ultimate cupcake recipe," buy special tools to decorate them perfectly, and then forget about those tools in a drawer somewhere because you've exhausted your interest in actually making the cupcakes.

Cooking can be a particularly pernicious source of toxic comparisons, especially given the number of people who like to photograph their meals and post the pictures. The renowned chef Edward Lee told me that the reason he didn't include any photos in his latest cookbook was because he didn't want his readers to tie themselves into knots trying to make the recipes look like professionally staged photos. Some people have told him that they tried his recipes but were disappointed because the finished dish looked terrible. "But did it taste good?" he asked them. "If it tastes good, that's all that matters."

That should be the new measure in most things: Is it good? Forget how it looks in photographs and ask yourself if you like it. Does it work? Instead of worrying about whether you stayed at the office longer than anyone else, focus on what tasks you accomplished and how well you completed them. Don't look at your friends' vacation photos and juxtapose them with your own. Instead, ask whether they enjoyed their time off.

It's natural to compare yourself to others, and it can be a source of inspiration. As I mentioned, comparisons can be motivating unless they are unrealistic. Chef Edward Lee's food has been carefully curated and manipulated by experts and photographed by professionals. Your dish probably won't look like the photos in cookbooks. Your selfie won't look like Gigi Hadid's, and your home shouldn't look like Kim Kardashian's.

If you're going to compare yourself to others, look only as far as your friends, family, and neighbors. Pardon the TLC quote, but don't search for a waterfall, "stick to the rivers and the lakes that you're used to."

It may seem naive to tell you to track your hours and look around instead of up, but these simple acts can be revolutionary. In the end, this is about reclaiming your time. It's about grabbing the reins so the horses are no longer driving you. However you want to describe it, taking control of your life begins with this elementary exercise. It is no more than stepping off the treadmill that's been exhausting you and taking you nowhere. It is one simple but powerful step.

Life-Back Three

STEP AWAY FROM YOUR DESK

The twentieth century will have to be fought all over again. But globally.

—DAVID SIMON

WHEN I WAS HOSTING a daily radio show in Atlanta, I regularly told my employees to go the hell home. I wrote a handbook for my producers that included the following advice: "Don't work a long day, go home, and turtle on your couch with a frozen dinner. Solid research shows forcing yourself to get out and go to the bar with friends, have dinner, see a movie, meet people and socialize, reduces your stress and makes you more efficient. Have a hobby." The guide also suggested that they leave the building for lunch and take a break every half hour or so.

It was nearly impossible for me to get my employees to follow this advice. Even with their boss walking by their desks, telling them to get up and go outside, even when I ordered them to go home, they still chose to put in sometimes ridiculous hours.

CEOs and executives at other companies have told me the same thing: They tell employees not to put in overtime and not to answer email on the weekends, but their workers continue to do it anyway. I don't know if those CEOs are being completely honest, but I guarantee that I was explicit about work hours with my staff. Ask them if you don't believe me. That's how ingrained is this idea that good employees and good people put in long hours.

It's time to work the hours you're required to work, and no more. Stop choosing to stay at your desk.

Obviously, this only applies to people who have some flexibility in their schedules and who find themselves answering emails and texts over the weekend. If you're working an hourly job and need every cent of your paycheck in order to make ends meet, working less is probably not possible. Sadly, there are far too many people in that situation in the industrialized world.

Under our current system, because we have so slavishly followed the dictums of corporate culture, income inequality is so high in the United States that working full-time is not enough to support two people, let alone a family. "Our economies [haven't] been shaped by our idea of fairness," writes Ethan Watters, author of *Crazy Like Us: The Globalization of the American Psyche.* "It was the other way around." Corporate values have seeped into nearly all areas of private life.

In 2016, the transportation company Lyft issued a celebratory press release about what they called "an exciting Lyft story." A driver named Mary went into labor while working and even picked up a fare on her way to the hospital. "Luckily, the ride was a short one," the press release added, with an implied wink.

My jaw dropped when I read that "adorable" story. Someone in the corporate office thought it was "cute" that one of their workers felt so much pressure to make a few extra dollars that she gritted her teeth, swallowed the pain of growing contractions, and kept driving. I think we can safely assume that working up until nearly the moment her baby was born was not part of Mary's birth plan.

I haven't spoken to Mary, and it's certainly possible that she wasn't in much pain and was delighted about how things turned out. I've talked to many drivers who love their jobs with Lyft and Uber. Maybe Mary views the events of that night as a cute story, much like Lyft does.

But this story is bigger than Mary, because it's a reflection of a global attitude about work-life balance. The reasons Mary might have felt compelled to stay in that car and pick up another fare are probably various. Many people work extra hours in order to cover medical expenses or to pay high rent or inflated car insurance bills. Those are not issues that any individual can solve on their own. Therefore, part of the solution must be political.

The current system in many industrialized nations is designed to force people to work long hours. Think for a moment about what you lose when you switch from full-time to part-time, at least in America. Your hours may be cut from forty to twenty, but the cost is much more than half of your income. You often lose healthcare and retirement benefits, plus sick time, vacation time, and family leave. Workers are heavily punished for cutting their hours. Why would that be, if not to feed the corporate appetite for time on the clock?

We will have to reevaluate our political priorities and decide whether we believe that working sixty to eighty hours per week is acceptable for an adult. According to data from MIT, a living wage in my neighborhood is more than $22 an hour. The average salary for a restaurant worker, landscaper, or salesperson is half that, and they generally get no sick days or paid vacation time. Do we think that's the kind of life our neighbors should lead? Is that the kind of life *we* want to lead? This is all part of a broader conversation we must have if we are to address the societal ills of overwork.

I would imagine that many people reading this book are not in that situation, though, and do have at least some flexibility in hours, some choice about whether to work in their off-time or not. If you are putting in more than forty hours a week in the office and answering emails at night or writing memos on the weekends, then you are most likely able to cut back without any broad policy changes or permission from your employers.

If your goal is less stress and more happiness, years of scientific research have proven that rather than trading your time for money, it's best to trade your money for time. In a study that gathered data from the United States, Canada, Denmark, and the Netherlands, researchers concluded that "buying time promotes happiness." In other words, paying others to mow your lawn, clean your car or house, or do your laundry is a great use of your money, even if it means you can't afford a bigger TV or an expensive vacation.

Buying time leads to much higher levels of life satisfaction, whereas feeling short on time leads to poor sleep patterns, anxiety, and less happiness, and is even linked to obesity, because people who feel they're too busy are less likely to exercise or eat well.

Surprisingly, there are some downsides to having more money in this instance, because wealthier people are more likely to spend their free time doing things that are ultimately stressful, like shopping and commuting. Because they don't get a chance to rest their mind, they are also more likely to feel they are pressed for time. The report states that "simply leading people to feel that their time is economically valuable induces them to feel that they do not have enough of it." When time is money and the amount of money goes up, we are more likely to think we can't afford to waste time.

I know it's irritating, when you are strapped for cash, to hear someone say that money can't buy happiness. And yet, above a certain income level, you are quite literally trading your health and happiness for a modest rise in pay (working excessive hours generally results in a pay raise of 6 to 10 percent). Once you reach a sustainable level of income, more money won't make you happier, but free time will.

Believe me, I'm not trying to tell you that money doesn't matter. It absolutely does, and poverty is associated with all kinds of negative outcomes. I've lived paycheck to paycheck for most of my life, just like the majority of Americans. In fact, 40 percent of Americans can't cover a $400 emergency expense without borrowing money, and I know from experience how stressful it is to be worried that something might happen that will throw your world into chaos.

I remember clearly, when I was a single mother working several jobs to meet my obligations, how proud I was to get $1,000 set aside in savings. That very week, someone stole my son's backpack from the park where he was playing with friends, and replacing the equipment and school books inside cost me $425. I was devastated, and so I understand on a personal level how exhausting it is to be always on the brink of disaster.

Even if you are living on the edge of financial stability, you may also be choosing to work extra hours, like I did, because you believe it will ultimately improve your situation. You may believe, like I did, that putting in unpaid hours will be noticed and rewarded.

But my income didn't ultimately go up because of extra hours in the office. My good fortune was not gifted to me by any grateful boss or manager. I got lucky when my TEDx Talk caught on. The talk was something that I chose to do in my spare time; I wasn't paid for it. Imagine if I had always invested my extra hours in myself and my creativity rather than in producing one more story for my company.

If your goal is to be happy, then working excessive hours may be taking you *further* from your objective of financial stability. What's more, if your goal is to be more productive, then your harried schedule is literally counterproductive.

We've known this for almost a hundred years, in fact. Back in the 1920s, Henry Ford noticed that when his employees worked too much, their productivity sank and the number of errors skyrocketed. That's why Ford decided to mandate an eight-hour day and a five-day week. "We know from our experience in changing from six to five days and back again that we can get at least as great production in five days as we can in six," he said. "Just as the eight-hour day opened our way to prosperity, so the five-day week will open our way to a still greater prosperity." Remember, Ford didn't invent the car. His greatest innovations were connected to increases in efficiency, and he simply discovered that long hours are inefficient.

Nearly a century later, Ford's conclusion has been proved correct over and over again. It is Parkinson's Law made plain: Work expands to fit the time available. So if you know you only have two hours to write an agenda, research shows that task will take two hours. If you have four hours to do it, that same task will suddenly require twice as much time. "General recognition of this fact," wrote C. Northcote Parkinson, for whom the law is named, "is shown in the proverbial phrase 'It is the busiest man who has time to spare.' "

Perhaps the reason long hours are unhelpful is that human brains are not designed to put in excessive hours of uninterrupted work. That was true for the employees on Ford's assembly line and it's doubly so for the knowledge workers of today.

In 1951, two men at the Illinois Institute of Technology kept track of nearly two hundred of their colleagues in the scientific and technical fields. They found that those who put in excessive hours were the least productive of all. After people passed a couple dozen hours in the lab, they saw decreasing returns on their labor. In fact, the most productive of the group were those who put in between ten and twenty hours a week, or two to five hours a day.

Still, we have designed our workplaces around the idea that long stretches of uninterrupted labor are productive. For more than two hundred years, we have tried to make human bodies and minds function like the machines we built or, more recently, like the computers we use. Do you remember the legend of John Henry? According to the folktales, the former slave John Henry was the strongest and most prolific steel driver on the Chesapeake and Ohio Railway. He dug his way through a mountain, legend tells us, to lay down the iron rails.

As the story goes, a man came by one day with a steam-powered drill. John Henry responded, according to the song, "A man ain't nothin' but a man, but before I let your steam drill beat me down, I'd die with a hammer in my hand." We're told that Henry *did* beat the steam drill, but he then fell down and died from exhaustion.

This, to me, is a classic story of the Industrial Revolution: A man dies to prove he's better than a machine. Historians mostly agree the legend of John Henry is probably based on a real person. Hundreds of African Americans perished while digging the Great Bend Tunnel in West Virginia, the site of the John Henry Historical Park, and they now lie uncelebrated and forgotten in unmarked graves near the tracks.

A steam drill or conveyor belt or computer can labor without rest, but humans need regular breaks. We don't persist; we pulse.

The human brain can accomplish incredible things when we give it the right environment in which to work. More and more, it's clear that the ideal schedule is short bursts of very focused work, followed by regular breaks. Research shows that if you work without interruption for fifty to fifty-seven minutes, then take a short break, you'll get much more done, and because you're more likely to engage the executive part of your brain while using this schedule, your work may be more insightful and creative.

Surveys have determined that the average person can focus for a few minutes shy of an hour, but remember that you are an individual and not an average. It's possible that your personal ideal is nearer to forty minutes or sixty minutes. This is something you'll have to test and discover for yourself.

It can be terrifying to experiment with shorter hours–I know from experience. Let me reassure you: Others have tried it and were successful beyond projections. We have real-world examples of organizations that have cut employee hours and experienced no reduction in productivity.

Remember the hospital in Sweden where administrators drastically cut hours for nurses and staff members? Everyone in the orthopedic unit worked six hours a day and no more than thirty hours per week, which is almost unheard of in the medical industry.

The administration was prepared to hire extra workers in order to make up for the reduction in hours, but was surprised to find that was unnecessary, as productivity didn't decrease. In fact, the executive director of the hospital told the *New York Times,* "The unit is performing 20 percent more operations, generating additional business from treatments like hip replacements that would have gone to other hospitals." And he said patients who once had to wait months for surgery now got into the operating room within a few weeks.

When you have fewer hours available to you, you automatically focus on the task at hand and ignore what's irrelevant. The quality of your work goes up as the allotted hours go down, so you can often accomplish more in four hours than in five.

Test this for yourself, like I did. Simply note the time when you start working, focus on one task at a time, and stop working when you become distracted or restless. Note that time down and keep track of your hours for a couple weeks. This process was illuminating for me and followed the current research on human attention spans almost perfectly.

I fell into the average, in that I could only focus for three or four hours at a time. Forcing myself to stand up and walk away, though, was difficult. I desperately wanted to keep going until everything was done and keep my nose to the proverbial grindstone. It required a nearly Herculean amount of effort to pry myself away at times, as I constantly told myself that working less supposedly equaled more productivity.

On average, I can only focus intently for a maximum of four hours a day. I also found that I needed a day off each week, sometimes two. Without those frequent breaks, I discovered that I was more easily distracted, more anxious, and more stressed.

Am I productive? I think so. I'm a very engaged single mother (my son would say *too* engaged) of a college freshman; I've written two books in less than three years, mostly while hosting a daily radio news show and delivering more than two hundred speeches in cities around the world. I have a very active social life that includes lots of barbecues and dinners out and walks through local parks. I'm as productive as I could possibly be, I think.

As you might expect, the amount of time you can sustain focused work varies widely from person to person. The MIT lecturer Robert Pozen recommends working for seventy-five to ninety minutes before resting. "That's the period of time," he told FastCompany.com, "where you can concentrate and get a lot of work done. We know that because we have studied professional musicians, who are most productive when they practice for this amount of time. It's also the amount of time of most college classes."

On the other hand, other experiments suggest the duration of uninterrupted work time should be significantly shorter. The software startup Draugiem Group tracked its employees' time and found the most productive among them worked for fifty-two minutes and then took seventeen-minute breaks, repeated throughout the day. In the report on that study, the researchers said the periods of working time were "treated as sprints for which [the most productive people] were well rested." As I've mentioned, I ended up in this group, needing to take a break about every fifty minutes or so.

You can split that time into smaller chunks, by the way, as long as you do one thing at a time. Spend twenty minutes on email, then call a coworker for ten, and then work on spreadsheets for another twenty before you get up and walk away.

In this age of distraction, though, we are rarely able to truly concentrate. There was an experiment conducted at the Berlin Academy of Music in which researchers tracked the practice habits of young musicians. This study was made famous years ago by Malcolm Gladwell and became the foundation for his theory that we have to put in 10,000 hours of practice before we truly master any skill.

One of the most interesting aspects of that study, I think, is the tendency among the best students to balance work hours with equivalent leisure. The study authors believe these young people have time to relax because they engage in what's called "effortful activities," or deliberate practice.

The psychologist K. Anders Ericsson says deliberate practice means "engaging with full concentration in a special activity to improve one's performance." This is not the relatively mindless chopping of vegetables or simply playing scales on a musical instrument over and over without cease. Instead, it is focused work in which the student is highly aware of their own performance, what they're doing wrong, and what they're doing right. They are mindful of what they're choosing to do to improve that performance and focus on drills that strengthen their weaknesses. As the study explains, "Many characteristics once believed to reflect innate talent are actually the result of intense practice extended for a minimum of 10 years."

The best students were not just hyperaware of how much time they spent in the practice room, though. They were also very accurate when estimating how much time they spent relaxing or socializing. They were mindful of how they spent their time overall, and they balanced work with regular periods of rest. They were intentional in their practice and in their idleness.

In other words, merely good musicians become great when they allow their brains to pulse, alternating focused work with intentional rest, and continuing that pattern for years at a time.

Sadly, most workers aren't really allowed to focus while they're on the job. We are often on a conference call while we're checking email and have eight tabs open in our browsers. Meanwhile, a friend is texting us about weekend plans and we're responding to notifications from Facebook. "We thrive on the feeling that we are some super task ninja, swatting all the incoming demands and messages in a hyper-efficient whirl," said the business psychologist Tony Crabbe in a piece for iNews.

Our general tendency to flit from task to task is well documented. A team at UC Irvine followed one group of workers for weeks and found that most people switch tasks about every three minutes. About half of the time, we are self-interrupted. For example, we'll work on a report for a few minutes and suddenly decide to look for something on Amazon or buy movie tickets or send a quick email to a friend.

It feels efficient when we switch tasks like this, but that efficiency is an illusion. Once you break your focus for any reason, it takes an average of twenty-three minutes to get back to full concentration.

What's more, we pay a cognitive "switch cost" every time we turn from our spreadsheet to our inbox to eBay and back. It may take less than a second to switch from one thing to the next, but eventually it all adds up to a lot of lost time.

Let's do the math: Imagine you're at work and at your computer for five hours out of the day. If you switch activities every three minutes, that's a total of one hundred interruptions, and you lose a second or so every time you do it. In the final tally, you lose up to 40 percent of your productive time to these switch costs. What's more, you're far more likely to make a mistake when you switch regularly. Your brain is not working at peak performance because it's constantly leaping from one thing to another.

This all suggests that creating an environment in which we can really focus will allow us to complete our work in less time. While managers tend to value lots of hours spent on the job, there's no evidence that working long hours results in better or more work. In fact, a professor at Boston University studied a large group of consultants and discovered that the managers couldn't tell the difference between people who actually put in eighty hours of work each week and those who pretended to. There was no discernible difference in their productivity.

The history professor Nelson Lichtenstein told me, "What you can't measure, you can't reward," and that may be why executives are so focused on work hours. For decades, the corporate world has been consumed with metrics. Managers love tangible measures by which they can determine success or failure. Work hours is one of the easiest ways to measure employee performance, but total hours worked is a meaningless statistic. In fact, while goal setting can be helpful, creating performance metrics for employees is often counterproductive.

Metrics can be useful and even enlightening, but if they are overused or even employed to measure things that are unmeasurable like innovation, metrics become destructive. Trying to meet numerical goals is also not particularly inspiring to the human mind, and so metrics don't encourage creative thought. Surveys reveal that 30 percent of knowledge workers claim they do absolutely no thinking while they're at work and nearly 60 percent say they do less than half an hour of thinking. It's fair to say that's an almost complete lack of mental stimulation.

Proving your worth by logging an arbitrary number of hours is more than silly—it's a practice that is killing productivity and, more seriously, endangering your health. Get up and get out.

Life-Back Four

INVEST IN LEISURE

> We work to have leisure, on which happiness depends.
>
> —ARISTOTLE

ONCE I REALIZED THAT I'd modeled my life after my workplace, I was dismayed to see how many of my choices were influenced by the corporate emphasis on efficiency. I saw it everywhere I looked.

I began by tracking my time and reducing my work hours, but it was clear that it would take much more than that to free myself. The effort to disentangle myself and create a clear delineation between job and home is ongoing. I'm like a tree that's grown next to a chain-link fence and now, decades later, find my roots and branches are enmeshed with the metal. To pull away now will require a gentle touch and plenty of patience.

For me, the next step was to address my addiction to multitasking. Not just address it, but end it. Trying to do several things at once instead of taking advantage of the brain's natural inclination to pulse between focus and rest is a waste of fertile brainpower. The structure of my work life consisted of hours spent at a computer or in meetings, switching from one task to another until it was time to stop. That structure was not designed for my human brain, and it had to be dismantled.

If you silence your phone, close your inbox, and really focus on getting a report done, research shows you'll finish 40 percent faster, have fewer errors, and have plenty of time to take a short walk around the building and let your brain relax.

Taking regular breaks is so important that it can't be left to chance or whim. I found I had to schedule leisure the way I schedule a yoga class or a business meeting.

There are two kinds of rest: leisure and time off, or spare time. Spare time is not true rest. As Sebastian de Grazia explains in his 1962 book, *Of Time, Work, and Leisure,* what we call "spare time" is the minutes and hours we find in between the work we do. It's inextricably tied to work and is meant to recharge our batteries so we can get back to work feeling refreshed.

Leisure, on the other hand, is separate from work. It should be unpolluted by work, meaning that you don't check your emails or answer work calls during this time, nor do you worry about how your activity might impact your work life. The purpose of leisure is not to make you better at your job, but to let you enjoy the life you work so hard to achieve.

However much time you spend in focused work, when it's time to get up and take a break, make sure you're really resting your brain. Don't text or do online shopping. Don't direct your thoughts toward any task at all. Downtime is healthy for the mind, and it's also an incredibly fertile neurological state.

When you're not directing your brain to do a specific task, your mind activates the default network.

The default mode network, or DMN, becomes active when we allow our minds to wander. When the DMN is engaged, it works on our memories, putting past events into context and making moral evaluations about things that have happened. It also imagines the future, tries to understand the emotions of others, and reflects on our own emotions and decisions. The default network is crucial for empathy, for self-reflection, and for Theory of Mind, the ability to imagine what others may be thinking.

Allowing our brains to switch into default mode is crucial for our well-being. That's the source of much of our creativity and innovation, since the brain actively reshuffles the puzzle pieces of our memories and emotions when it's not directed to solve a problem or complete a task.

In practice, your brain will only switch to default mode if you allow it to ramble without purpose. It's not idleness, since you could be jogging or wiping down counters during this time.

The psychologists Amanda Conlin and Larissa Barber warn that we often misuse our breaktime during work hours. "One key component of an effective break is psychological detachment," they wrote in *Psychology Today,* "which refers to mentally disengaging from work thoughts. By shifting our focus, detachment helps us to directly reduce work demands that are causing fatigue and to naturally recover."

If you decide to call a loved one or friend during your break, resist the temptation to talk about work. Make a clean break. Certainly, don't walk into your office kitchen and spend fifteen minutes talking to a coworker about the job. Take a breath and hit pause. I was amused to read a tweet from the media strategist Stu Loeser that said, "I am sitting on an Acela [train] next to someone who is sitting with her hands on her lap, quietly looking out the window. No computer out. No tablet out. No phone out. Just peacefully looking out at the world as we pass it by. Like a psychopath would." My answer to Stu: "I am sometimes that psychopath."

When you're not at work, you can actually enjoy not just time off but true leisure. You can be completely detached from concerns about work, and you should strive to make a complete separation. I realize it feels necessary to answer emails and texts promptly, but that habit is incredibly hard on your body and mind.

Research shows employees who feel more detached from their jobs during their time at home are emotionally healthier and more satisfied with their lives. They're less likely to feel emotionally exhausted, and they report getting better sleep.

I think that of all the changes I recommend, this is the easiest to achieve. I only ask that you take it easy and relax, and that you schedule time out of every day in which to do this. As the economist Joseph Stiglitz says, we learn how to enjoy leisure "by enjoying leisure."

Set aside a chunk of time every day to do nothing productive. Take a walk without a destination and without worrying about the number of steps you'll take. Go outside. Group walks in nature lower stress and decrease symptoms of depression, so walk through a park.

I often put my phone into Do Not Disturb mode for hours at a time and allow only calls and texts from friends and family to come through. The work calls can, and do, wait. I have even started setting aside one day per week as an "untouchable day," when I don't look at my email inbox or social media and simply go about my day without interruption.

Every Monday, I don't check social media or email and texts. I'll pick up the phone if someone calls, but almost no one does. Since starting this practice, I've gotten better at shutting out distractions and using that day for writing and other tasks that require focus. But the first few weeks were rough, I have to admit.

On my first untouchable day, I checked my email more than fourteen times. Twice, I didn't even realize that I was doing it until someone sent me an email saying, "Aren't you supposed to be off of email today?" The truth is, my life was centered around email in more ways than I realized.

Although I'd turned off notifications from almost all of the apps on my phone, I was still seeing that number of unread items next to the envelope icon every time I glanced at the screen. What's more, my internet browser included the email page in its startup screens, so the inbox opened automatically.

Depending on which research you consult, the average adult spends two to six hours a day answering email and at least a third of that isn't urgent. I'd imagine much, much more than a third is neither important nor time sensitive. I could cite studies and surveys all day, but it comes down to this: Email kills productivity. So breaking my addiction to it was crucial if I wanted to really get things done on my untouchable day.

Still, I found I could not address the problem in isolation. I also had to reckon with the expectations of others. People expect a quick response. At this point, anything less than immediate response over text or email is cause for concern. Most texts are read within three minutes of being received, and the most common email response time is two minutes, according to analysis from the University of Southern California's Viterbi School of Engineering.

Here's how I've solved (most of) these problems. First, on Sunday night I check my email one last time and turn on a vacation responder that says, "On Mondays, I don't answer emails or texts because I'm writing. If it's urgent, call me." By the way, it's been nearly a year and no one has ever called.

Second, I changed my email signature in order to manage response time expectations. Now, instead of a pithy quote, all of my messages end with the following note: "I only check email 2–3 times a day. If it's urgent, call me. But how urgent is it, really?" Over time, I hope people will stop expecting an immediate reply from me and will feel more comfortable when it takes hours, if not days, to receive a reply.

Third, I changed the settings on my phone so that I no longer see how many unread emails are in my inbox, and every Monday, I put the phone on Do Not Disturb mode so that only phone calls come through.

The result? During one of my untouchable days, I wrote 4,000 words before my brain overheated. Then I baked some scones and took my dog for an hour-long walk, and still had time to watch some Netflix before reading a book and falling asleep at a reasonable hour. I slept well, too.

I know it's scary to lift your foot off the gas pedal, but trust me that you'll enjoy the ride much more. You don't need a special app or a guide from an expert to "hack your leisure time." Sometimes striving to improve on everything we do can impede progress. Stop becoming and just be for a moment.

You certainly don't have to take a walk. It's often my choice but doesn't have to be yours. You can choose to watch a movie while your phone is turned off or sit at a coffee shop and read a novel. Do a puzzle or a crossword, work on your car, or just take a hot bath and listen to music. Whatever it is that you like to do when you have nothing on your calendar, do it and don't think about work.

There's even scientific evidence that shows watching cat videos is good for you. A growing body of evidence suggests that quality leisure time, meaning leisure time that is truly disengaged from work concerns, will ultimately make you better at and more satisfied with your job. "Productivity science seems like an organized conspiracy to justify laziness," wrote Derek Thompson in the *Atlantic*. He calls the findings on leisure and vacation and cute animal videos "nearly too good to be true."

Work is necessary and can be fulfilling when you feel a sense of purpose in what you do, but it is not the justification for your existence. Remember that we are not biologically and evolutionarily "born to work."

We are, however, designed to relate with other people and form intimate bonds with friends and family. While work is a tool used to gain other necessary things, belongingness is a fundamental need. That's why it's important to also set aside time to be social.

Life-Back Five

MAKE REAL CONNECTIONS

Alone, we can do so little; together, we can do so much.

—HELEN KELLER

IT'S OKAY TO FOCUS on yourself, to reflect on what you need, to invest in your future. It's equally important to spend time strengthening your community.

If you spend an hour or two on social media every night, set aside some of that time to meet someone for coffee or attend a concert. It's possible you feel you don't have the time or energy to do so, but that may be because you're unknowingly wasting it online. If you have only two hours' worth of social energy each day, you can either spend that time arguing with someone on Facebook or hanging out with a friend.

Don't think about these face-to-face meetings as a waste of your time; they are, in fact, an incredibly good use of time. Lack of social connection is even associated, at times, with less money. When you feel happy, you are more likely to make positive connections with other people, and those connections can lead to increased income. People who are less lonely often have more income.

The social psychologist Gillian Sandstrom is an expert in social interactions and conversations. She and Elizabeth Dunn ran an experiment in 2014 that found many people often avoid chats with grocery store clerks and baristas because they're in a hurry. And yet, we enjoy a lot of benefits if we take a minute to strike up those conversations. "In the current study," wrote Sandstrom and Dunn, "people who had a social interaction with a barista (i.e., smiled, made eye contact, and had a brief conversation) experienced a more positive effect than people who were as efficient as possible." That's why they ultimately titled the report "Is Efficiency Overrated?"

We persistently resist the impulse to chat, though, and I'm not entirely sure why. I traveled to the United Kingdom and spent a few days with Dr. Sandstrom in order to figure out why we avoid the social interaction that we desperately need. Sandstrom is trying to answer that question too, and believes it may be fear and anxiety that prevent people from reaching out. So she is running an experiment in the hopes that she can train people to talk to strangers and therefore increase their level of comfort with social interaction.

For the experiment, study participants are assigned missions every day through a specialized mobile app. Those missions direct them to compliment someone on their sweater or talk to a person wearing glasses. Participants were required to talk with no fewer than four strangers over the course of a week.

I sat in on a training session for the experiment and asked the people there if they thought they would find it difficult to converse with four strangers a week. Most (more than 80 percent that I spoke to) said yes. Yet I later spoke with several people who had already completed the experiment, and they all said they enjoyed it and found it easy. One student, Amber Brad, said she was disappointed at first to find that she had to talk to people in person instead of texting them, but ended up having a good time. "You can't really express emotions through text," she told me. "Things can be taken the wrong way."

Another student, Donnell Perkins, agreed with her: "Texting is not a real conversation. There are so many emotions that come up in conversation. I got a mood boost from the longer conversations I had. I even tried to extend those talks because I enjoyed them more." I was fairly surprised to hear these sentiments from young people, since 75 percent of millennials would rather have a phone that can only text than one that only makes phone calls.

I heard echoes of these sentiments again and again when I spoke with people who'd already completed Dr. Sandstrom's experiment. These are roughly the same results researchers have found during experiments around the globe: People generally expect to hate talking with people in person and on the phone, but enjoy it when they're forced to do it. That's why it's important that you force yourself to do it.

Unfortunately, our lives are no longer designed to accommodate social interactions. Our cars have become tiny living spaces, our phones allow us to distance ourselves from others, even our homes have become bubbles that we rarely have to leave. The ratio of lot size to home size has declined over the past few decades as people added more space inside and stopped spending time outdoors.

One staff member at the University of Essex told me the experimental game had encouraged her to finally speak to some of her neighbors. Mandy Fox, a project officer in human resources, told me she'd seen several of the people on her street before, working in their gardens or walking their dogs, but she'd never spoken to them. "The game gave me an excuse to say hello, and I've talked briefly with several of them since," she told me. "And the same thing happened with the janitor at my daughter's school. I've seen him dozens of times, standing just a few feet away from him and never saying a word. I talked to him for the experiment and now we chat every time I see him."

If it's true that many of us need an excuse to start conversations with strangers or to talk with neighbors, I give you full permission to use me as your excuse. Tell them you're required to talk with someone every day, if that helps. Chat with your coworkers and your taxidriver. You may dread small talk, but study after study shows that those conversations make you healthier, happier, and more relaxed. The benefits of authentic social interaction are immediate and primal. Set aside some time to talk with friends or make sure that you make contact with strangers when you're out and about.

In this day and age, it's unlikely that other people will strike up a conversation with you on the elevator or the subway, so take the initiative and say good morning. As the behavioral scientist Nicholas Epley has said, few people wave, but almost everyone waves back.

Humans are so biologically primed to take benefit from social encounters that we get a bump to our mood and mental health even when a stranger simply makes eye contact and nods as they pass us on the street. Just that small gesture—a smile or a nod or a wave—helps you feel more connected to your community. That brief hello from someone on the elevator can make you feel as though you belong.

These brief interactions are no replacement for long-lasting relationships, of course, and will not truly fulfill your need for belongingness, but they will make you feel better and less stressed. They also may encourage you to invest more in either finding a confidant or spending more time with the close friends you have.

If you take away nothing else from this book, I hope you understand that human beings are at their best when they are social, and human minds work best in connection with other human minds. It may not be the most efficient way to live, but it's the most likely to foster well-being.

Join a club, go to a book talk at your library or bookstore, sign up for a group hike at a local park. It may sound old-fashioned to become a member of a bowling league or a Rotary club, but those kinds of social networks can quite literally save your life. My son spends every Saturday playing complicated board games with his friends at a local gaming café.

Playing cards with your cousin might seem silly, and gossiping with an old school friend might seem frivolous, but socializing regularly can add as many years to your life as quitting smoking. Avoiding social contact is making us sicker, and seeking it out will make us healthier. It really is that simple.

Work in Teams

Because human beings are beautifully designed to work in conjunction and collaboration with other humans, the next change you should make is to work in teams whenever possible. Perhaps the most effective solution to our modern obsession with productivity and efficiency is to tap in to the human hive mind. In the words of Rudyard Kipling, "The strength of the pack is the wolf, and the strength of the wolf is the pack." It may sound cool to be a "lone wolf," but real lone wolves don't survive as long.

We have evolved to think in groups and bounce ideas off others. Analysis of data from diverse industries going back decades shows that even the most experienced expert reaches better conclusions when their recommendations are merged with the advice of less-knowledgeable people.

Brainstorming, or generating new ideas, is often best done alone, when people can focus in quiet. But the process of evaluating those ideas and choosing the best path forward should be a group activity. Study after study shows that groups of people outperform individuals on a wide range of tasks, from math to linguistic problems to business decisions. Groups of three to five students repeatedly outperformed even the smartest individuals, and they were less prone to mistakes.

Oddly, we tend to do the opposite in the working world. We call brainstorming meetings in order to generate new ideas and then return to our offices to decide which idea will best suit our needs. This practice should be flipped on its head. Brainstorm alone and evaluate or analyze as a group. A good rule of thumb is that diverse groups who are allowed to make decisions independently will outperform even the most expensive consultant.

We often decide to make decisions alone because we feel it's more efficient. "Design by committee" is a common insult, used to describe a project that's flawed and uninspired because it included the input of too many people. Most of us have had some experience with meetings at work in which coworkers shot down good ideas, quibbled over meaningless details, or consistently supported the safest option.

The error in these situations, though, was not in gathering input from many people but in trying to reach consensus without minimal conflict. Consensus is about being comfortable and avoiding arguments, but comfort is the enemy of innovation.

Cognitive diversity is disconcerting to many people because it almost always brings differing opinions, but it is essential for creative problem-solving and accuracy. It is what our big *Homo sapiens* brains are designed to respond to and exploit.

Again and again, we've seen that better decisions are made by polling all employees of an organization than by relying on the judgment of a CEO or one executive team. "However well-informed and sophisticated an expert is, his advice and predictions should be pooled with those of others to get the most out of him," James Surowiecki says in his book *The Wisdom of Crowds*. "The more power you give a single individual in the face of complexity and uncertainty, the more likely it is that bad decisions will get made."

Most businesses are not set up to gather the opinions of all employees, though, so how might this look in practice? Let's say you're deciding on a venue for an annual conference. You ask the members of your team to send their ideas, so they're coming up with proposals independently. Then you gather those ideas and sift through them as a group. Research shows you'll then make the best choice by polling everyone you can. Send out a mass email and ask everyone to vote. That increases your chances of getting the best decision.

Here's the bottom line: The average of answers from a large, independent, and diverse group of people will often be more accurate than the answer arrived at by a smart individual or a small group of smart people. In our culture, which focuses on personal achievement and sometimes worships charismatic individuals like Steve Jobs or Elon Musk, this advice can seem counterintuitive, but it's backed by decades and decades of evidence from a wide variety of industries.

I know it feels more efficient to work alone, but the point of this book is to encourage you to ask more questions about efficiency. Does your current process really save time, or are you taking that on faith? Are you hoping merely to save a little time or to do the best work, find the best solution, live your best life?

It's essential that we ask these kinds of questions so we can clearly articulate our goals instead of blindly investing in strategies and tools that promise to improve our lives but don't explain what's being improved or what the end result will be. Let's be honest: I'm not sure most of us have stopped to consider what our larger goals are. There's no time for that.

One Kind Act

The world can be a cruel place, so it might surprise you to know that science has proven, over and over, that humans are mostly kind. Kindness is intuitive for the vast majority of us, and given the choice to treat people well or treat them badly, we generally choose the former. Goodwill is human and natural.

It turns out, we are most likely to be unkind when we overthink things and get wrapped up in our own thoughts, our own issues. Since self-absorption is a global phenomenon at this point, it can be useful to intentionally break that pattern and reestablish habitual kindness.

So, if you truly want to break free of the obsession with efficiency, practice random acts of kindness. I'm not telling you this because I think it's the moral or nice thing to do (even if it is). I'm telling you to do this because years of research proves that doing nice things for other people, even small things, is incredibly good for you. As the psychotherapist and Jesuit priest Anthony de Mello wrote: "Charity is really self-interest masquerading under the form of altruism."

Humans are biologically incentivized to be kind to each other, and we're rewarded by our bodies when we do it. Committing a selfless act triggers a release of endorphins, the neurotransmitters that help block feelings of pain and even create a euphoric sensation. Altruism can produce the same elation as vigorous exercise, an effect that's sometimes called the "helper's high."

There may be a physical benefit as well, since people who volunteer regularly tend to live longer and be healthier. There are a great many variables that might affect this finding, though, so it's not possible to know the precise nature of the connection. It could be that the types of people who volunteer are also more active or less likely to engage in risky behaviors like smoking. Still, there is a connection between altruism and physical health that we simply don't understand yet.

Another significant benefit, especially for those who are driven and busy, is that focusing on someone else's needs helps to distract you from what's going wrong in your own life. As long as what you do for another is not so difficult or time-consuming that it becomes overwhelming, a random act of kindness can be healing during times of stress.

The link between kindness and happiness is not new. It's been a theme of literature and morality tales for hundreds of years, and many of us watch it play out again every year through some version of Charles Dickens's tale of Ebenezer Scrooge. A study from the 1980s demonstrated that families who donated their deceased loved one's organs felt better and less depressed. Even people who suffered from chronic pain or cancer found they felt better after helping someone else.

In an article for the *International Journal of Behavioral Medicine,* the author Stephen G. Post reviews the scientific case for kindness and points to an evolutionary connection. "Anthropologists discovered that early egalitarian societies (such as the bushmen) practice institutionalized or 'ecological altruism,'" Post wrote, "where helping others is not an act of volunteerism but a social norm. Perhaps those of us in contemporary technological cultures are isolated in various respects and have strayed too far from our altruistic proclivities." Perhaps this is one more negative side effect of our increasingly isolated lives.

Kindness is certainly good for others and good for society, but I'll let others make the ethical case for generosity. Here, I'm focused on the benefits to the agent of altruism, not the target. I would argue that doing one small selfless act every day could reduce your stress significantly and increase your well-being.

While you are making your checklist of things to do, just include one act of kindness, no matter how small, and you may eventually see a significant impact on your stress level and health. The person you're kind to, by the way, is also more likely to be kind to someone else.

Imagine this: You're in the drive-through getting lunch and you decide to pay for the person behind you as well. That means they are more likely to pay for the person behind them. It also means that you're all helping each other to break away from a cultural emphasis on individual needs and ultimately reengage your instinctive (and kind) human nature. That's a pretty big bang for your buck.

Life-Back Six

TAKE THE LONG VIEW

> When it is obvious that the goals cannot be reached, don't adjust the goals, adjust the action steps.
>
> —CONFUCIUS

ONE DAY LAST YEAR, I was driving to the movies with my son and a small car pulled in front of us. On the back bumper was a sticker with a quote from J.R.R. Tolkien's *Lord of the Rings* books: "Not all who wander are lost." My son read it, considered it, and then said, "You can tell that was written a long time ago because people don't wander anymore. We have GPS now."

I thought he was being facetious at the time, but looking back, I realize he was simply speaking the literal truth: We rarely go anywhere now without finding the fastest, most efficient way to reach our destination. It has become easier than ever to be specific about our goals and to reach them quickly. In many ways, we have become a goal-oriented culture. Wandering, or even getting lost, are old-fashioned activities.

I don't long for the days when I had to stare at a street atlas looking for the tiny side street where a friend lived and then figure out how to get there, but I do wonder if we've become as addicted to the process of setting goals as we are to our smartphones. Perhaps we are due for a reconsideration of how we choose our goals and how we choose to reach them.

Ends, Not Means

The truth is, productivity is a by-product of a functional system, not a goal in and of itself. The question is not whether you are productive but what you are producing.

I suspect our hunger for increased productivity and efficiency is good. We are never done improving. That's the upside. It's telling that in the Declaration of Independence, we are guaranteed not happiness but the "pursuit of happiness." We are always chasing it. We never stop tweaking and twisting our lives in search of more free time, more money, more satisfaction.

In some cases, though, we are indiscriminate about our methods. We make decisions in the moment without considering where that decision might ultimately take us. We deny ourselves desserts and long vacations because we believe that these small decisions will bring us closer, even incrementally, to a nebulous goal. If I just spend thirty minutes answering email tonight, that means it will be easier tomorrow, right? (You know the answer to that.)

Answering emails in the evening is the means to a goal. It is an activity you can choose to engage in, but it's not a real objective. No one's goal in life, as far as I know, is to answer every email within twenty minutes. So before you pick up your phone or tablet at nine p.m. and check your inbox, ask yourself what your true intention is. If you choose not to work during evenings and weekends, what might happen?

The truth is, going without dessert is a means goal, as is making your bed every day, getting up at five a.m., or answering email before bed. All of these activities are *means to an end.* They are meant to be stepping-stones toward a more significant aim, like achieving life satisfaction or improving the world.

Means goals are specific objectives, like a certain income or job title, that lead to a bigger, greater goal. They are tools used to reach a more fulfilling intention.

Perhaps you think a bigger salary will help you achieve stability, and that will bring happiness. Maybe you think a promotion will bring you more power in the office, allowing you to create better products and feel useful to society. In those cases, your end goals are happiness and being of use to the wider world, not more money and more power.

It's important to ensure your choices are really helping you progress as you want them to. Will your promotion bring you the power you need or not? Before you invest a lot of hours in pursuing that new position, make sure it's worth it.

Many of us become obsessed with means goals and completely lose sight of the more important end goal that should motivate all our efforts: living a good life. Why sacrifice your mental and physical health for something that may not help you and, in fact, takes you further from your ultimate ambition?

End goals are non-negotiable. We don't compromise on end goals, because we are unwilling to accept something less than a happy family or living an honorable life. Means goals are flexible. If your family can't be happy in Texas, you'll live in California. The location of your home is a means to an end.

Let's say your end goal is to experience the beauty of nature and therefore enrich your life. So you have a means goal to visit the Grand Canyon this year. There's a contest to win a free trip and you enter twenty times, but you ultimately lose the contest. That doesn't matter, though, because you can still get to Arizona. And if you can't, you can probably still visit a place that is beautiful and spiritually enriching. Winning the contest is a means goal, but people often confuse means and ends and get overly attached to the means. They lose the contest and think, *Oh well, I guess I wasn't meant to visit the Canyon.*

End goals often provide a direction—going west—instead of a specific destination. You may need to travel south a bit to get gas or food, but then you return to your westward path. If you want to lose weight, your target weight is a means goal. Reaching a certain number on the scale isn't your ultimate goal, or probably shouldn't be.

The real aim may not even be to look better if what you really want is to be healthier or more physically capable. If the means goal is to train until you can run a marathon, perhaps the end goal is to live longer and be more able-bodied.

In an effort to make us all more efficient at reaching goals, some experts have offered systems for setting them. For example, many recommend the SMART system, which suggests that good goals are specific, measurable, actionable, realistic, and time-bound.

That system is useful but has limits, for goal-setting is a multilayered exercise. I set a goal of writing no fewer than 750 words per day while working on this book, for example. That was the means by which I reached my goal of finishing the manuscript. Finishing it was the means by which I reached the goal of relaying to people a message that I think can be helpful. And *that* was a means by which I hope to reach one of my end goals: making the world a better place.

Perhaps you notice that "making the world a better place" is not specific, measurable, or time-bound. It is an end goal and will therefore not fit into the SMART system. Many end goals don't, but means goals do. Steve Pavlina, author of *Personal Development for Smart People,* says, "End goals work as ideals to move towards, and one of the reasons they must transcend the limits of a system like S.M.A.R.T. is that they must be expansive enough that you can pursue them for a lifetime." As I said, end goals are often directions instead of destinations. They are not usually items you can include in a checklist or bullet journal.

Focusing on ends rather than means is helpful because it leads us to find creative solutions to problems (if not this way, then another way). It also can reduce stress, because it embraces failure and welcomes flexibility.

If you fail to meet a means goal, there are usually dozens of other methods to reach your overriding objective. Failing is itself a productive method to reach your broader aim through a process of elimination. Thomas Edison famously said that he never failed but "found 10,000 ways that won't work."

So your challenge is to articulate your end goals, knowing that they may change as time passes. Why are you going to college? To earn a degree, but why do you want a degree? In order to get a good job, and why do you want that? You can use a version of Sakichi Toyota's "Five Whys." Keep asking yourself *why* until you ultimately arrive at your fundamental objective.

If you don't articulate your end goals, it can be easy to waste your time doing things that you think are good and productive but that don't actually help you progress. A lot of the advice we get these days tells us to aim for arbitrary measures, like 100,000 followers or spending an hour at the gym every day. We live by our checklists and notifications telling us to drink more water.

We've been told for decades to focus on specific, achievable targets. I'm not telling you to throw those targets away but to make sure those targets lead you to bigger and better things. This will save you time and money and prevent you from doing things that feel productive but achieve nothing in the long run.

In truth, we sometimes set means goals too quickly. We read an article on how to be more productive that tells us that all successful CEOs wake up early, so we vow to get up at five a.m. every day. Then we feel like a failure when we sleep until seven o'clock. Perhaps a coworker recommends a paleo diet and we start following it with a vague idea that it will make us healthier, until we break down and eat some pizza. This knee-jerk approach can cause us to try a lot of different strategies without thorough consideration or analysis.

Choosing means goals in haste can waste a vast amount of time. You solve this problem by starting on the other end of the spectrum. Articulate your end goals and then choose smaller, specific goals that you are reasonably sure will bring you closer to the bigger objective. Check in frequently to make sure your habits truly are helping you make progress. If they're not, don't waste any more time on them. Dump them and try something else.

Realize that everything you do is likely just a means to a larger goal. These tasks are not commandments but suggestions. They are fluid and flexible. They are negotiable and can be seen as lines in sand, not stone. If you fail to reach a means goal, there's no need to get stressed or anxious. Just find another way to reach your ultimate aim.

So here is the complete list of solutions, all designed to break your addiction to efficiency without purpose and productivity with production.

---

1. Increase time perception.
2. Create your ideal schedule.
3. Stop comparing at a distance.
4. Work fewer hours.
5. Schedule leisure.
6. Schedule social time.
7. Work in teams.
8. Commit small, selfless acts.
9. Focus on ends, not means.

This list may represent small tweaks to your current habits, or it could be that following these guidelines will require a massive overhaul. Regardless, learn from my experience and start with one at a time. Most things are good for you only up to the point where they become oppressive and overwhelming. I certainly don't recommend that you turn this list into another productivity hack that causes further stress.

All of these actions are backed by science and by my own personal experience and research. They will probably work for you. But if they don't, or if it's not possible to carry out one of them, that's perfectly fine. The point of all this is to simplify your life and increase well-being, not create another source of anxiety.

In one sense, every one of these suggestions is really about time management, but not in pursuit of more efficiency. The overriding message is this: Stop trading time for money. The simple act of placing a value on an hour has made us loath to waste even a minute, and the more money you have, the more expensive your time is and the more you feel you don't have enough time to spare. Our perception of time is now horribly warped.

Leisure becomes stressful when you subconsciously believe you are wasting money by not being productive. However, if one of your end goals is to be happy, then pursuing a bigger income is not necessarily going to get you where you want to go. Allow yourself to consider other options.

It's time to stop viewing your off-hours as potential money-making time. It's not worth it. You can't put a monetary value on your free time, because you're paying for it in mental and physical health.

Do not let corporate values determine how you spend your days and what your priorities are. You are a big-brained, social animal who's currently constrained by unrealistic demands and expectations. Your vision has been narrowly focused for too long on your work and your marketability, but your intrinsic value as a human is more related to your position in your community than to your earning power as a laborer.

Stop trying to prove something to others. Reclaim your time and reclaim your humanity.

CONCLUSION

> We have changed our environment more quickly than we know how to change ourselves.
>
> —WALTER LIPPMANN

I REMEMBER VERY CLEARLY the day that my mother got her first microwave. My mom was a widow, raising four kids by herself, and while I could debate many of her parenting choices, I would never deny that she worked hard. For her birthday one year, my eldest sister suggested that we all chip in to buy her a microwave.

It must have been the late 1970s, since I was eight and probably didn't contribute much to the purchase. I was the youngest of the bunch. My sister bought the microwave and wrapped it and I still remember our shared excitement as we watched our mother open it.

That machine was incredible! It took just a couple minutes to heat a can of soup in the microwave, instead of ten or fifteen on the stove. It also required fewer dishes, since you could pour the soup into the same bowl you would eat from, instead of using a saucepan. Even at my young age, I knew that device would save my mother a lot of time, and I also knew that my mom never reached the end of her to-do list.

Looking back, though, it took significantly less time for my mother to go about her daily chores than it did for my grandmother. My grandmother dried clothes on a line in the yard and made coffee in a saucepan before straining it through a sieve. She used tooth powder instead of paste in a tube and mended her stockings when they snagged. My great-grandmother didn't have a refrigerator and bought ice from an iceman.

In a very short period of time, life has become immeasurably easier and less time-consuming. We tend to take these conveniences for granted until an appliance breaks down, when we suddenly realize how much we depend on our washing machine or our central heating unit.

I have no doubt that we humans will continue to improve our lives, because the drive to make things better is innate. Leave a group of people alone at a specific location for a significant length of time and they will inevitably start working to improve the living conditions or their own quality of life.

Consider for a moment how much higher our standards are now than they were just a hundred or so years ago. In widely cited research into expertise, researchers in the United States and Belgium noted that it's harder than ever to reach the rank of "expert" in many fields. "The fastest time for the marathon in the 1896 Olympic Games," they wrote, "was just a minute faster than the required entry time in large marathon races such as the Boston Marathon [in 1990]."

Even in fields where expertise is harder to measure than in a race, the modern practitioner outpaces his or her recent ancestors. "When Tchaikovsky asked two of the greatest violinists of his day to play his violin concerto, they refused, deeming the score unplayable," the study report says. "Today, elite violinists consider this concerto part of the standard repertory." Scientists claim that even the legendary violinist Paganini, whose skill was so phenomenal that people called him "the Devil's violinist" and "the Virtuoso of Virtuosos," would "cut a sorry figure if placed upon the modern concert stage."

This is all to say that striving to improve and attain ever higher levels of performance is not a bad impulse. We are precocious animals. Humans have always worked to achieve more than their parents and grandparents; that impulse has served us well.

However, we have stagnated in many areas and even lost ground in measures like infant mortality, income equality, and environmental safety. Our effort to institutionalize progress, to turn it into a metric and measure it, is now interfering with our ability to create it. Human innovation and invention, it turns out, can't be weighed and dissected and forced.

We try to force innovation in much the same way that we try to manufacture creativity. In the past few decades, as industrialized nations transitioned from economies largely dependent on manufacturing to ones that rely mostly on knowledge workers, a new emphasis on creativity emerged. The OECD (Organisation for Economic Cooperation and Development) urged educators to "cultivate the creativity and critical thinking skills of students."

But it's difficult, if not impossible, to create programs that specifically increase the creative drive, and equally tricky to track creativity. How do you know if a child has become more creative over the course of a school year? How can that be measured? The author Ephrat Livni commented that leaders don't seem much interested in letting creativity "develop independently. Instead, it is being quantified, dissected and tested, taught and measured."

Creativity is at the heart of all innovation, invention, and progress and is, therefore, a critical skill. Yet it cannot be increased through long hours of work or massive doses of caffeine or specially designed computer equipment. Creativity cannot be institutionalized. Most of the time, new innovations are developed in order to solve problems, not because someone set aside time to "be creative." The key is to create an environment in which the brain is most likely to access its creativity.

Many people are focused now on happiness, perhaps because so many people are unhappy. Economic growth, it turns out, is not connected to human happiness or even increased health. Russia has seen incredible economic growth over the past two decades, and yet Russians are dying at an earlier age now than they did during Soviet rule. Life expectancy has fallen by 40 percent there since the 1980s. "A rising tide can indeed lift a variety of boats," John Cacioppo and William Patrick write in the book *Loneliness,* "but in a culture of social isolates, atomized by social and economic upheaval and separated by vast inequalities, it can also cause millions to drown."

Millions are drowning now.

Let me be perfectly plain: Working harder will not solve this problem. We've talked about changes that can help individuals. Now let's talk about solutions that might be able to help the world.

Let's first finally put an end to the myth of the "self-made man." No one, man or woman, achieves fabulous success using only their wits and hard work, not even in fiction. Everyone has help and a little bit of luck. Rags-to-riches fairy tales might convince you that if you just work a little harder and want something a little bit more, you will rise to incredible heights. If you just sacrifice your weekends and wake up at five every day, you will get the big house and the important job title with the great salary. What comes after that, whether it's bliss or euphoria, is anyone's guess.

Many people who are now CEOs and millionaires have worked very hard, no question, but so have millions of people now living below the poverty line. Hard work is admirable, but statistics show it is not a magic potion that will transform your life.

Historians have noted that the specter of the "self-made man" served an important capitalist purpose: It allowed those in power to control the narrative that motivated workers. John Swansburg, deputy editor of the *Atlantic,* says mythologized stories about Ben Franklin and Andrew Carnegie served "as an explanation for success and for failure. If success were a function of a man's good character, then failure must be evidence that his character was weak." Therefore, fear of judgment compelled many people to put in more and more hours so they might be deemed "deserving." The self-made-man fairy tale is part of a shaming culture.

Remember that Andrew Carnegie, the man who said, "Do your duty and a little more and the future will take care of itself," was the same man who fought vigorously to maintain a twelve-hour workday for the steelworkers he employed. Few jobs are as physically demanding or dangerous as those in the steel mills of the early twentieth century.

We accept many things in our lives without question, believing this is "how it's done." It's time to reevaluate many of the principles and priorities that govern our lives. The self-made-man ideal is just one of them.

Another is the pursuit of constant growth in the consumer economy. Constant growth is not possible, and yet our jobs, retirement funds, and national financial security require growth to be considered healthy. As Kate Raworth said in her 2018 TED Talk, "We have economies that need to grow, whether or not they make us thrive, and what we need, especially in the richest countries, are economies that make us thrive whether or not they grow."

Globally, we are not merely addicted to growth in stock markets and profit margins and GDP. It's not just about bigger salaries that bring bigger houses and cars, either. We have absorbed this worship of constant growth into our very psyches. We believe we can and should be constantly working toward our individual improvement, constantly tinkering and improving ourselves. We believe there is no crest on this mountain.

While it may feel that the forces that have brought us to this era of distraction—time pressure, intense productivity, and obsessive efficiency—are too strong and pervasive to be countered, the truth is that the demand for long hours and forced productivity is relatively recent. The past two hundred years are a mere blink in the long stare of our species' evolution. We can choose to return to a style of living that's more likely to help us thrive.

We can develop new habits that better suit our innate need to belong, our thirst for companionship, and our ability to imagine incredible things through a focused mind. To bring about this new paradigm will require a substantive change in our personal priorities and, ultimately, new economic priorities and policies as well.

It is past time to let go of the idea that we deserve stability and comfort only if we spend most of our waking hours at work. Is this how we want our children and future generations to live, or do we wish for them more space to breathe, to relax, to reflect, to enjoy the company of others? What is the world we envision for ourselves and the ones we love?

Ultimately, this is an ethical question. In a study published in the *Journal of Business Ethics,* the psychologists Tim Kasser and Kennon Sheldon laid out the evidence showing that higher pay doesn't result in a happier life and pondered what to do with that information. Most companies, after all, are built around the opposite principle, and so they reward workers with pay raises and bonuses. They punish offenders with reduced hours, fines, and sometimes total loss of compensation through termination.

"Given that financial rewards can undermine the intrinsic motivation and enjoyment that comes from pursuing activities," Kasser and Sheldon ask, "is it ethical for companies to reward employees primarily with financial raises and bonuses?" Is it ethical to judge the worth of an individual based on the person's salary? Is the highest-paid employee always the smartest, the most creative, the most productive?

I think the answer is clearly no. Human beings are social animals who are at their best when they connect with one another. Collaboration is our superpower. Perhaps we can create a culture in which relationships are prioritized instead of productivity. Human beings have a great capacity for joy. I would love to see us make joy a goal.

I started this project because I was trying to improve my own life, and I have done that. The change in my daily routine is immense. Even my doctor commented on the drop in my cortisol levels. I am less anxious than I was a year ago, and no less productive. On a personal level, the research has been useful and the experiment successful.

But in the end, this isn't really about me. It wasn't my choices, ultimately, that overloaded my schedule. It was the hard-work culture that made me believe I was lazy if I stopped working for even short periods of time. So the solution cannot come from my choices but from a collective choice to change the paradigm.

There is one aspect of early human history I hope we can reclaim: a celebration of what is most human about us. It is our reflective thought and social connections that make us unique and strong. Descartes said, *"Cogito ergo sum"*: I think, therefore I am. He did not say, *"Laboro ergo sum"*: I work, therefore I am.

More than two hundred years ago, the rules were rewritten. It's time to rewrite them again.

ACKNOWLEDGMENTS

I WORK IN INDUSTRIES where one or two people are recognized for work done by hundreds of others as a team. This is true in radio and in opera, and it's also true in book publishing. Many thanks to my agent, Heather Jackson, who called me out of the blue one day in 2016 and said, "Hey, do you think you could write a book?" Her support and friendship have lifted me to heights I'd never dreamed of. Thanks to my wonderful editor, Michele Eniclerico, who understood what this book was about from the beginning and has worked so hard to make it good. Thanks to the entire team at Harmony Books and Penguin Random House.

Thank you to the many brilliant people who made time to answer my questions and have dedicated their careers to understanding the world and helping others understand as well: Silvia Bellezza, Juliana Schroeder, Nelson Lichtenstein (who stuck with me despite a horrible connection while I was riding the train), Rachel Simmons, Jared Yates Sexton, Graeme Maxton, Roy Baumeister, Nicholas Epley, and Adam Grant. Many, many thanks to my friend Gillian Sandstrom, who let me spend a few days with her in Colchester, watching her research project.

Thanks to Pete, who doesn't read my books but is always willing to talk through difficult topics; to Carol, who understands and travels the book journey with me; to Beth, who met me in Chicago while I was riding the train around the country; to Doug, who's been a rock in my life for almost twenty years.

I happen to have the best team in the entire world and they don't complain when I screw up and send a work email over the weekend: Ashley and Kayce at Triple 7, Alexis, and the inimitable Cynthia Sjoberg, who is the best partner and friend anyone could ask for. Everyone should have a Cynthia in their life.

Thank you to my best friend, Theresa. There's so much to be grateful for in our friendship and your support. And, most of all, thank you to my son. He knows why, because I annoy him by telling him all the time.

NOTES

Introduction

xiv "Our level of happiness may change": Alex Lickerman, "How to Reset Your Happiness Set Point," *Psychology Today,* April 21, 2013.

xiv "the only animal whose desires": Henry George, *Progress and Poverty* (New York: D. Appleton & Co, 1879), 98.

xvi We chose not to take 705 million vacation days: U.S. Travel Association, "State of American Vacation 2018," May 8, 2018.

xvi And yet research reveals that what most parents actually want: Lucia Ciciolla, Alexandria S. Curlee, Jason Karageorge, and Suniya S. Luthar, "When Mothers and Fathers Are Seen as Disproportionately Valuing Achievements: Implications for Adjustment Among Upper Middle Class Youth," *Journal of Youth and Adolescence* 46, no. 5 (May 2017): 1057–75.

xvii Suicide rates among teens: Jean M. Twenge, Thomas E. Joiner, Mary E. Duffy, A. Bell Cooper, and Sarah G. Binau, "Age, Period, and Cohort Trends in Mood Disorder Indicators and Suicide-Related Outcomes in a Nationally Representative Dataset, 2005–2017," *Journal of Abnormal Psychology,* March 14, 2019.

xviii "I can hunch over my computer screen": Dan Pallotta, "Worry Isn't Work," *Harvard Business Review,* August 20, 2010.

xix The Greeks work more hours: "Average annual hours actually worked per worker," Stats.OECD.org.

xix "Leisureliness": Linton Weeks, "Lazy in America: An Incomplete Social History," NPR.org, July 1, 2011.

Chapter 1: Mind the Gap

6 "We are enslaved by speed": "The Slow Food Manifesto," *SlowFoodUSA.org.*

10 "Slow travel now rivals": Carl Honoré, "In Praise of Slowness," Ted.com, July 2005.

Chapter 2: It Starts with a Steam Engine

15 "as just part of their daily activities": Allison George, "The World's Oldest Paycheck Was Cashed in Beer," *New Scientist,* June 22, 2016.

18 medieval peasants worked no more than eight hours a day: James E. Thorold Rogers, *Six Centuries of Work and Wages: The History of English Labour* (London: M. P. Swan Sonnenschein, 1884).

18 "The age had its drawbacks": Ibid., p. 69.

18 most serfs owed "day-a-week": Henry Stanley Bennett, *Life on the English Manor: A Study of Peasant Conditions, 1150–1400* (Cambridge: Cambridge University Press, 1937).

19 "The laboring man will take his rest": Juliet B. Schor, *The Overworked American: The Unexpected Decline of Leisure* (New York: Basic Books, 1992).

23 "Companies now needed workers' time": Tony Crabbe, "A Brief History of Working Time—And Why It's All About Attention Now," inews.co.uk, April 18, 2017.

24 Paul Revere was an accomplished silversmith: Nelson Lichtenstein, interview with the author, June 28, 2018.

25 in 1858, an article first used *efficiency* to mean: *Online Etymology Dictionary,* s.v. "efficiency," accessed July 30, 2018.

27 "crazy, tumble-down old house": John Forster, *The Life of Charles Dickens* (London: Virtue & Co, 1876), 10.

27 "The Industrial Revolution ultimately": Rick Bookstaber, "Class Warfare and Revolution (Circa 1850)," Rick.Bookstaber.com, November 8, 2011.

28 "to recover what his ancestor": Thorold Rogers, *Six Centuries of Work and Wages.*

31 "In the last months of the year 1918": Stephen Bauer, "The Road to the Eight-Hour Day," *Monthly Labor Review,* August 1919.

31 "An alarming number of workers": Stanley Aronowitz and William DiFazio, *The Jobless Future* (Minneapolis: University of Minnesota Press, 2010), 336.

Chapter 3: Work Ethic

34 "Remember that *time* is money": Benjamin Franklin, "Advice to a Young Tradesman," in George Fisher, *The American Instructor: Or Young Man's Best Companion,* 9th ed. (Philadelphia, 1748), quoted in Max Weber, *The Protestant Ethic and the Spirit of Capitalism,* trans. Talcott Parsons (New York: Charles Scribner's Sons, 1958), "The Spirit of Capitalism," ch. 11, p. 48.

35 "My theory of self-made men": Frederick Douglass, "Self-Made Men," a lecture from 1872, available at monadnock.net/douglass/self-made-men.html.

36 "His Excellency is certainly": Quoted in Anne Curzan, "Just Try That with Your Bootstraps," *Chronicle of Higher Education,* March 7, 2017.

37 "Beliefs in the American Dream": Michael W. Kraus and Jacinth J. X. Tan, "Americans Overestimate Social Class Mobility," *Journal of Experimental Social Psychology,* May 2015.

37 A separate study from Princeton revealed: Martin V. Day and Susan T. Fiske, "Movin' On Up? How Perceptions of Social Mobility Affect Our Willingness to Defend the System," *Social Psychological and Personality Science,* November 22, 2016.

38 nearly 70 percent of citizens believe: Pew Charitable Trusts, "Economic Mobility and the American Dream—Where Do We Stand in the Wake of the Great Recession?" May 2011.

38 "Is it a healthy myth that inspires": John Swansburg, "The Self-Made Man: The Story of America's Most Pliable, Pernicious, Irrepressible Myth," *Slate,* September 29, 2014.

39 "When asceticism was carried out": Weber, *The Protestant Ethic and the Spirit of Capitalism,* 181.

39 "until the last ton": Ibid.

40 "Work is our sanity": Henry Ford, *My Life and Work* (Garden City, NY: Doubleday, Page, Garden, 1923), 74.

40 experts predict that by 2035: Allen Downey, "The U.S. Is Retreating from Religion," *Scientific American,* October 20, 2017.

40 "Our society measures personal worth": Rebecca Konyndyk DeYoung, *Glittering Vices: A New Look at the Seven Deadly Sins and Their Remedies* (Grand Rapids, MI: Brazos Press, 2009).

41 "For the first time since his creation": John Maynard Keynes, *Economic Possibilities for Our Grandchildren* (1930; repr., London: Palgrave Macmillan, 2010).

42 "This prediction is not so much": Karl Widerquist, "John Maynard Keynes: Economic Possibilities for our Grandchildren," *Dissent,* Winter 2006.

43 "By the late 1950s": Schor, *The Overworked American.*

43 "when we reach the point": "Prof. Huxley Predicts 2-Day Working Week," *New York Times,* November 17, 1930.

44 "The benefits of productivity": Nelson Lichtenstein, interview with the author, June 28, 2018.

45 "The Greatest Generation thought": Jared Yates Sexton, interview with the author, July 3, 2018.

46 "If anything, time is used": Gary S. Becker, "A Theory of the Allocation of Time," *Economic Journal* 75, no. 299 (September 1965): 493–517.

Chapter 4: Time Becomes Money

48 Consider for a moment this experiment: Sanford E. DeVoe and Julian House, "Time, Money, and Happiness: How Does Putting a Price on Time

Affect Our Ability to Smell the Roses?" *Journal of Experimental Social Psychology,* July 14, 2011.

49 "Ever since a clock was first used": "Why Is Everyone So Busy?" *Economist,* December 20, 2014.

50 "The more cash-rich": Magali Rheault, "3 in 10 Working Adults Are Strapped for Time in the U.S.," *Business Insider,* July 20, 2011.

50 when it comes to sheer number of hours: "Hours Worked," Data.OECD .org.

50 A number of agencies in Europe: Eurofound, "Work-Related Stress," *European Foundation for the Improvement of Living and Working Conditions,* November 21, 2010.

50 The productivity expert Laura Vanderkam: Laura Vanderkam, *Off the Clock: Feel Less Busy While Getting More Done* (New York: Portfolio, 2018).

50 "yuppie kvetch": Daniel S. Hamermesh and Jungmin Lee, "Stressed Out on Four Continents: Time Crunch or Yuppie Kvetch?" *Review of Economics and Statistics,* May 2007.

51 "many American employees are near": "Study: U.S. Workers Burned Out," ABC News, May 16, 2001.

51 the payroll services company Paychex: "Workplace Stress Is on the Rise," Paychex, March 1, 2017.

51 "overworked, pressured, and squeezed": Bronwyn Fryer, "Are You Working Too Hard?" *Harvard Business Review,* November 2005.

52 "cyberslacking": Roland Paulsen, "The Art of Not Working at Work," *Atlantic,* November 3, 2014.

53 "Polluted time": Josh Fear, "Polluted Time: Blurring the Boundaries Between Work and Life," Australia Institute, November 19, 2011.

54 Plus, it's likely that Tiny Tim's ailment: Stephanie Pappas, "Dickensian Diagnosis: Tiny Tim's Symptoms Decoded," *LiveScience,* March 5, 2012.

57 "unifying faith of industrial civilization": Christopher Ketcham, "The Fallacy of Endless Economic Growth," *Pacific Standard,* May 16, 2017.

57 "We have this 'common sense' belief": Graeme Maxton, interview with the author, July 11, 2018.

58 "Parents are devoting less attention": Schor, *The Overworked American,* p. 5.

59 "We actually could have chosen": Ibid., p. 2.

61 "If you find yourself": Max Nisen, "18 People Whose Incredible Work Ethic Paid Off," *Business Insider,* October 11, 2013.

61 "Everyone wants to be a model employee": Dan Lyons, "In Silicon Valley, Working 9 to 5 Is for Losers," *New York Times,* August 31, 2017.

62 "Working nineteen hours a day every day": Gary Vaynerchuk, "The Straightest Road to Success," GaryVaynerchuk.com, 2015.

62 "One of my colleagues said of another": Jared Yates Sexton, interview with the author, July 3, 2018.

63 "It's easy and alluring to say to yourself": Dorie Clark, "The Truth Behind the 4-Hour Workweek Fantasy," *Harvard Business Review,* October 4, 2012.

64 "Don't tell me that there's something": Daniel Heinemeier Hansson, "Trickle-Down Workaholism in Startups," *SignalvNoise,* May 30, 2017.

66 "For years, we've been told": Liz Alderman, "In Sweden, an Experiment Turns Shorter Workdays into Bigger Gains," *New York Times,* May 20, 2016.

67 "Work has become more than work": Silvia Bellezza, interview with the author, June 15, 2018.

67 "creating zones of privacy": Ethan S. Bernstein, "The Transparency Paradox: A Role for Privacy in Organizational Learning and Operational Control," *Administrative Science Quarterly,* July 2012.

69 "Leisure": Henry Ford, "Why I Favor Five Days' Work with Six Days' Pay," *World's Work,* October 1926, interview by Samuel Crowther.

69 In the 1800s, many European governments: Sheldon Garon, "Why We Spend, Why They Save," *New York Times,* November 24, 2011.

70 "The biggest gift that the United States could get": Larry Light, "Why Holiday Shopping Is So Important for the U.S. Economy," CBS News, November 28, 2016.

70 "The answer to America's economic problems": Roger Simmermaker, "Why Buying American Can Save the U.S. Economy," *New York Times,* September 16, 2011.

72 "conspicuous abstention from labor": Thorstein Veblen, *The Theory of the Leisure Class: An Economic Study of Institutions* (1899; repr., Oxford: Oxford University Press, 2007), ch. 3, "Conspicuous Leisure," p. 30.

72 someone wearing a Bluetooth headset: Silvia Bellezza, Neeru Paharia, and Anat Keinan, "Conspicuous Consumption of Time: When Busyness and Lack of Leisure Time Become a Status Symbol," *Journal of Consumer Research,* June 2017.

73 "Leisure held the first place": Veblen: *The Theory of the Leisure Class,* ch. 3, "Conspicuous Consumption," p. 74.

73 "harried leisure class": Staffan B. Linder, *The Harried Leisure Class* (New York: Columbia University Press, 1970).

74 "The average consumer": Lorenzo Pecchi and Gustavo Piga, eds., *Revisiting Keynes: Economic Possibilities for Our Grandchildren* (Cambridge, MA: MIT Press, 2010).

75 "When people are paid more": Becker, "A Theory of the Allocation of Time," 493–517.

76 "When I was a kid": Graeme Maxton, interview with the author, July 11, 2018.

76 A survey of golfers in 2015: Michael Roddy, "A Round of Golf Takes Too Long to Play, Survey Finds," Reuters, April 27, 2015.

77 "One reason over a trillion dollars a year": J. R. Benjamin, "Is There a Universal Human Nature?" *The Bully Pulpit* (blog), February 22, 2013.

Chapter 5: Work Comes Home

79 "the cult of efficiency from office to home": Arlie Russell Hochschild, *The Time Bind* (New York: Henry Holt and Co., 1997), 50.

82 "What I see is that we've taken": Andrew Taggart, "Life Hacks Are Part of a 200-Year-Old Movement to Destroy Your Humanity," *Quartz,* January 23, 2018.

83 even when the computer is used only to take notes: Pam A. Mueller and Daniel M. Oppenheimer, "The Pen Is Mightier Than the Keyboard: Advantages of Longhand over Laptop Note Taking," *Psychological Science,* April 23, 2014.

84 "The research is unequivocal": Susan Dynarski, "Laptops Are Great. But Not During a Lecture or a Meeting," *New York Times,* November 22, 2017.

84 "We adopt the illusion": Taggart, "Life Hacks Are Part."

86 "could be applied with equal facility": Scott Cutlip, *The Unseen Power: Public Relations, a History* (Hillsdale, NJ: Lawrence Erlbaum Associates, 1994), 168.

86 "Those who manipulate this unseen mechanism": Edward Bernays, *Propaganda* (Brooklyn: IG Publishing, 1928), 9–10.

87 "The most pernicious thing": Oliver Burkeman, "Why You Feel Busy All the Time (When You're Actually Not)," BBC.com, September 12, 2016.

88 "The goal was never to be idle": Tim Ferriss, "24 Hours with Tim Ferriss: A Sample Schedule," Tim.blog, March 10, 2008.

89 "Maybe all the time I spend": John Pavlus, "Confessions of a Recovering Lifehacker," Lifehacker.com, May 29, 2012.

90 "The courts are empty": Myron Medcalf and Dana O'Neil, "Playground Basketball Is Dying," *ESPN,* July 23, 2014.

91 membership has declined: Peter Lewis, "Unions, Clubs, Churches: Joining Something Might Be the Best Act of Resistance," *Guardian,* November 22, 2016.

91 Parents are now afraid: "Why Is Everyone So Busy?"

92 "type of introspective thought process": Mary Helen Immordino-Yang, Andrea McColl, Hanna Damasio, and Antonio Damasio, "Neural Correlates of Admiration and Compassion," *Proceedings of the National Academy of Sciences,* May 12, 2009.

92 conserve our "psychic energy": Georg Simmel, *The Metropolis and Mental Life* (Brooklyn: Wiley-Blackwell, 1903).

Chapter 6: The Busiest Gender

95 we are slower at completing tasks: American Psychological Association, "Multitasking: Switching costs," *APA.org,* March 20, 2006.

96 "Heavy multitaskers" have the same trouble: Ira Flatow, "The Myth of Multitasking," *Talk of the Nation*, NPR, May 10, 2013.

97 "suggest that women might find it easier": S. V. Kuptsova et al., "Sex- and Age-Related Characteristics of Brain Functioning During Task Switching (fMRI Study)," *Human Physiology,* August 18, 2016.

98 "Because the first thing": Patti Neighmond, "Study: Multitasking Multi-stressful for Working Moms," *Morning Edition*, NPR, December 2, 2011.

98 "These women worked like crazy in school": Larissa Faw, "Why Millennial Women Are Burning Out at Work by 30," *Forbes,* November 11, 2011.

100 "Gwen's stories are more like situation comedies": Arlie Russell Hochschild, *The Time Bind* (New York: Henry Holt and Co., 1997), 12.

103 "[She] came to my room": Carol Lloyd, "Grade Grubbing: When Parents Cross the Line," GreatSchools.org, June 21, 2018.

104 men stay on the job for about: Danielle Paquette, "Men Say They Work More Than Women. Here's the Truth," *Washington Post,* June 29, 2016.

106 "Men feel more satisfied": Niharika Doble and M. V. Supriya, "Gender Differences in the Perception of Work-Life Balance," *Management,* Winter 2010.

106 "One of the worst career moves": Claire Cain Miller, "The Motherhood Penalty vs. the Fatherhood Bonus," *New York Times,* September 6, 2014.

110 working moms are *less* stressed: Sarah Damaske, Joshua M. Smyth, and Matthew J. Zawadzki, "Has Work Replaced Home as a Haven? Re-examining Arlie Hochschild's *Time Bind* Proposition with Objective Stress Data," *Social Science and Medicine,* August 2014.

Chapter 7: Do We Live to Work?

113 "Work becomes the object in itself": Davide Cantoni, "The Economic Effects of the Protestant Reformation: Testing the Weber Hypothesis in the German Lands," *Journal of the European Economic Association,* November 24, 2014.

113 "rewards, punishments, or obligation": Cody C. Delistraty, "To Work Better, Work Less," *Atlantic,* August 8, 2014.

114 "I can't have downtime": Rachel Simmons, "Why Are Young Adults the Loneliest Generation in America?" *Washington Post,* May 3, 2018.

114 "idleness is potentially malignant": Christopher K. Hsee, Adelle X. Yang, and Liangyan Wang, "Idleness Aversion and the Need for Justifiable Busyness," *Psychological Science,* July 2010.

115 "A lot of people derive meaning": Andrew Taggart, "Our 200-Year-Old Obsession with Productivity," *International Policy Digest,* February 6, 2018.

115 "I don't know *how* to retire": Ann Brenoff, "So Why Are Baby Boomers Still Working?" *HuffPost,* May 15, 2018.

116 "Hard work is the only way forward": Lorenzo Pecchi and Gustavo Piga, eds., *Revisiting Keynes: Economic Possibilities for Our Grandchildren* (Cambridge, MA: MIT Press, 2010).

117 damage caused by *not* having a job: Gordon Waddell and A. Kim Burton, *Is Work Good for Your Health and Well-Being?* (London: Stationery Office, 2006).

117 even the most urgent of issues at work: Shankar Vedantam, "When Work Becomes a Haven from Stress at Home," *Morning Edition,* NPR, July 15, 2014.

118 Still, we know that for every extra year: Carole Dufouil et al., "Older Age at Retirement Is Associated with Decreased Risk of Dementia," *European Journal of Epidemiology,* May 4, 2014.

118 Consider this updated list of human needs: Nicole Gravagna, "What Are Fundamental Human Needs?" *Quora,* November 6, 2017.

121 "If you look at energy consumed": J. Aguilar et al., "Collective Clog Control: Optimizing Traffic Flow in Confined Biological and Robophysical Excavation," *Science,* August 17, 2018.

122 "We're not focusing on the right thing": "Workers Embrace Four-Day Week at Perpetual Guardian," *NZ Herald,* March 30, 2018.

125 "The first person who thought of putting": Fred Gratzon, *The Lazy Way to Success: How to Do Nothing and Accomplish Everything* (Fairfield, IA: Soma Press, 2003), 43.

126 link between a lack of activity and deeper thinkers: Todd McElroy et al., "The Physical Sacrifice of Thinking: Investigating the Relationship Between Thinking and Physical Activity in Everyday Life," *Journal of Health Psychology,* January 20, 2015.

126 Decades of research demonstrate: John Kounios and Mark Beeman, "The Aha! Moment: The Neural Basis of Solving Problems with Insight," *Creativity Post,* November 11, 2011.

127 "Once you start daydreaming": Manoush Zomorodi, "What Boredom Does to You," *Nautilus,* October 23, 2018.

127 "could be the crux of what makes humans different": Ibid.

Chapter 8: Universal Human Nature

130 "There is something biologically given": "Human Nature: Justice Versus Power," a debate between Noam Chomsky and Michel Foucault, 1971, Chomsky.info./1971xxxx.

132 nearly all research subjects used for studies: Jeffrey J. Arnett, "The Neglected 95%: Why American Psychology Needs to Become Less American," *American Psychologist,* October 2008.

135 can identify their cry: James A. Green and Gwene E. Gustafson, "Individual Recognition of Human Infants on the Basis of Cries Alone," *Developmental Psychobiology,* November 1983.

136 he asked people to listen: Michael W. Kraus, "Voice-Only Communication Enhances Empathic Accuracy," *American Psychologist,* October 2017.

136 "So people were accurate": Carey Goldberg, "Study: To Read Accurately How Someone Is Feeling, Voice May Be Best," *CommonHealth,* WBUR.org, October 10, 2017.

137 claims we spend about fifty-five: TextRequest, "How Much Time Do People Spend on Their Mobile Phones in 2017?" Hackermoon.com, May 9, 2017.

139 had one student tell a story about a fiasco: Greg J. Stephens, Lauren J. Silbert, and Uri Hasson, "Speaker-Listener Neural Coupling Underlies Successful Communication," *Proceedings of the National Academy of Sciences,* August 10, 2017.

140 researchers taught monkeys to pull a chain: Roy Baumeister and Mark R. Leary, "The Need to Belong: Desire for Interpersonal Attachments as a Fundamental Human Motivation," *Psychological Bulletin,* May 1995.

141 "Belongingness needs do not emerge": Ibid.

141 Forty-two married couples: Janice K. Kiecole-Glaser et al., "Hostile Marital Interactions, Proinflammatory Cytokine Production, and Wound Healing," *Archives of General Psychiatry,* December 2005.

142 "Without sustained social interaction": Atul Gawande, "Hellhole," *The New Yorker,* March 23, 2009.

143 "The empathy of our closest evolutionary": Frans de Waal, "Does Evolution Explain Human Nature?" John Templeton Foundation, April 2010, templeton.org/evolution/Essays/deWaal.pdf.

145 declines in empathy have been recorded: Paula Nunes et al., "A Study of Empathy Decline in Students from Five Health Disciplines During Their First Year of Training," *International Journal of Medical Education,* February 1, 2011.

146 "Chimps," Frans de Waal says, "would fight": Frans de Waal, email interview with the author, May 9, 2018.

149 "Just because we have a capacity": De Waal, "Does Evolution Explain Human Nature?"

Chapter 9: Is Tech to Blame?

153 when we pick up tools: Ed Yong, "Brain Treats Tools as Temporary Body Parts," *Discover,* June 22, 2009.

155 "I think a lot about how jobs": Jared Yates Sexton, interview with the author, July 3, 2018.

156 "The nanosecond is a billionth": Schor, *The Overworked American.*

158 Ninety-five percent of them: Nathalie Cohen-Sheffer, "Text Message Response Times and What They Really Mean," *Rakuten Viber* (blog), November 6, 2017.

158 When scientists at Harvard tested: "Blue Light Has a Dark Side," *Harvard Health Letter,* August 13, 2018.

159 Many apps are meant to engage your mind: Jessica C. Levenson et al., "The Association Between Social Media Use and Sleep Disturbance Among Young Adults," *Preventive Medicine,* April 2016.

159 the more interaction you have with your phone: Myriam Balerna and Arko Ghosh, "The Details of Past Actions on a Smartphone Touchscreen Are Reflected by Intrinsic Sensorimotor Dynamics," *Digital Medicine,* March 7, 2018.

160 brain splits the two sides into two separate teams: Sylvain Charron and Etienne Koechlin, "Divided Representation of Concurrent Goals in the Human Frontal Lobes," *Science,* April 16, 2010.

160 The mere presence of a smartphone: Christian P. Janssen et al. "Integrating Knowledge of Multitasking and Interruptions Across Different Perspectives and Research Methods," *International Journal of Human-Computer Studies,* July 2015.

161 participants were told how zippers work: Matthew Fisher, Mariel K. Goddu, and Frank C. Keil, "Searching for Explanations: How the Internet Inflates Estimates of Internal Knowledge," *Journal of Experimental Psychology,* March 30, 2015.

162 "I am convinced the Devil lives": Nellie Bowles, "A Dark Consensus About Screens and Kids Begins to Emerge in Silicon Valley," *New York Times,* October 26, 2018.

162 Steve Jobs famously did not allow: Nick Bilton, "Steve Jobs Was a Low-Tech Parent," *New York Times,* September 10, 2014.

164 "Our minds are not designed to allow us": Susan Pinker, *The Village Effect* (Toronto: Vintage Canada, 2014).

165 "We're trying to make the text-based medium": Juliana Schroeder, interview with the author, June 19, 2018.

166 more people want to quit social media: Ella Alexander, "More People Want to Quit Social Media Than Smoking in 2017," *Harper's Bazaar,* January 4, 2017.

166 "hijacks our psychological vulnerabilities": Tristan Harris, "How Technology Hijacks People's Minds—from a Magician and Google's Design Ethicist," medium.com/thrive-global/how-technology-hijacks-peoples-minds-from-a-magician-and-google-s-design-ethicist-56d62ef5edf3.

167 "diaper product": Haley Sweetland Edwards, "You're Addicted to Your Smartphone. This Company Thinks It Can Change That," *Time,* April 13, 2018.

170 "Many young adults turn to the screen": Rachel Simmons, "Why Are Young Adults the Loneliest Generation in America?" *Washington Post,* May 3, 2018.

Life-Back One: Challenge Your Perceptions

176 "Resilient systems": Roger L. Martin, "The High Price of Efficiency," *Harvard Business Review,* January–February 2019.

Life-Back Two: Take the Media Out of Your Social

189 Researchers discovered that many people imagine: Sebastian Dori, Shai Davidai, and Thomas Gilovich, "Home Alone: Why People Believe Others' Social Lives Are Richer Than Their Own," *Journal of Personality and Social Psychology,* December 2017.

190 "obsessed with creating a perfect artifact": Jared Yates Sexton, interview with the author, July 3, 2018.

190 "The first draft is the child's draft": Anne Lamott, *Bird by Bird* (New York: Anchor Books, 1995).

191 "the home has been turned into part of the market": Rachel Simmons, interview with the author, July 3, 2018.

191 "American students are increasingly being sorted": Steven Singer, "Middle School Suicides Double as Common Core Testing Intensifies," *HuffPost,* August 2, 2017.

193 "But did it taste good?": Edward Lee interview with the author, *1A*, NPR, July 2, 2018.

Life-Back Three: Step Away from Your Desk

196 "Our economies [haven't] been shaped": Ethan Watters, "We Aren't the World," *Pacific Standard,* February 25, 2013, psmag.com.

198 "buying time promotes happiness": Ashley V. Whillans et al., "Buying Time Promotes Happiness," *Proceedings of the National Academy of Sciences*, August 8, 2017.

200 "We know from our experience": Ford, "Why I Favor Five Days' Work with Six Days' Pay."

201 "General recognition of this fact": C. Northcote Parkinson, *Parkinson's Law* (London: John Murray, 1958), 4.

201 They found that those who put in excessive hours: Raymond Van Zelst and William Kerr, "Some Correlates of Technical and Scientific Productivity," *Journal of Abnormal and Social Psychology,* October 1951.

202 Historians mostly agree the legend: Paul Garon, "John Henry: The Ballad and the Legend," *The New Antiquarian,* the blog of the International League of Antiquarian Booksellers, December 14, 2009.

203 "The unit is performing": Liz Alderman, "In Sweden, an Experiment Turns Shorter Workdays into Bigger Gains," *New York Times,* May 20, 2016.

204 "That's the period of time": Stephanie Vozza, "This Is How Many Minutes of Breaks You Need Each Day," *FastCompany,* October 31, 2017.

205 "treated as sprints for which": "Desktime for Productivity Tracking," DraugiemGroup.com, December 2017.

205 experiment conducted at the Berlin Academy of Music: K. Anders Ericsson, Ralf Th. Krampe, and Clemens Tesch-Römer, "The Role of Deliberate Practice in the Acquisition of Expert Performance," *Psychological Review,* July 1993.

206 "We thrive on the feeling": Tony Crabbe, "A Brief History of Working Time—And Why It's All About Attention Now," inews.co.uk, April 18, 2017.

207 In the final tally: American Psychological Association, "Multitasking."

208 managers couldn't tell the difference: Erin Reid, "Why Some Men Pretend to Work 80-Hour Weeks," *Harvard Business Review,* April 28, 2015.

208 "What you can't measure": Nelson Lichtenstein, interview with the author, June 28, 2018.

Life-Back Four: Invest in Leisure

211 "One key component of an effective break": Amanda Conlin and Larissa Barber, "Why and How You Should Take Breaks at Work," *Psychology Today,* April 3, 2017.

212 Research shows employees who feel more detached: Sabine Sonnentag, "Psychological Detachment from Work During Leisure Time: The Benefits of Mentally Disengaging from Work," *Current Directions in Psychological Science,* March 2012.

215 watching cat videos is good for you: David Cheng and Lu Wang, "Examining the Energizing Effects of Humor: The Influence of Humor on Persistence Behavior," *Journal of Business and Psychology,* December 27, 2014.

215 "Productivity science seems like an organized conspiracy": Derek Thompson, "A Formula for Perfect Productivity: Work for 52 Minutes, Break for 17," *Atlantic,* September 17, 2014.

Life-Back Five: Make Real Connections

217 "In the current study": Gillian Sandstrom and Elizabeth W. Dunn, "Is Efficiency Overrated?: Minimal Social Interactions Lead to Belonging and Positive Affect," *Social Psychological and Personality Science,* September 12, 2013.

219 few people wave: Nicholas Epley, *Mindwise* (New York: Knopf, 2014), 70.

221 "The strength of the pack is the wolf": Rudyard Kipling, "The Law for the Wolves," in *A Victorian Anthology, 1837–1895,* ed. Edmund Clarence Stedman (Boston: Houghton Mifflin, 1895).

222 "However well-informed and sophisticated": James Surowiecki, *The Wisdom of Crowds: Why the Many Are Smarter Than the Few and How Collective Wisdom Shapes Business, Economies, Societies, and Nations* (New York: Anchor Books, 2004), 220.

224 "Charity is really self-interest masquerading": Anthony de Mello, *Awareness* (New York: Image Books, 1992).

225 families who donated their deceased loved one's organs: Helen Levine Batten and Jeffrey M. Prottas, "Kind Strangers: The Families of Organ Donors," *Health Affairs,* Summer 1987.

225 "Anthropologists discovered that early egalitarian": Stephen G. Post, "Altruism, Happiness, and Health: It's Good to Be Good," *International Journal of Behavioral Medicine,* 2005.

Life-Back Six: Take the Long View

231 "End goals work as ideals to move towards": Steve Pavlina, "End Goals vs. Means Goals," StevePavlina.com, August 23, 2005.

Conclusion

237 "The fastest time for the marathon": Ericsson, Krampe, and Tesch-Römer, "The Role of Deliberate Practice in the Acquisition of Expert Performance."

238 "cultivate the creativity and critical thinking": Stéphan Vincent-Lancrin, "Teaching, Assessing, and Learning Creative and Critical Thinking Skills in Education," *Organisation for Economic Cooperation and Development,* oecd.org/education/ceri/assessingprogressionincreativeandcriticalthinking-skillsineducation.htm.

239 "develop independently": Ephrat Livni, "The Cult of Creativity Is Making Us Less Creative," *Quartz,* November 7, 2018.

239 "A rising tide can indeed lift a variety": John T. Cacioppo and William Patrick, *Loneliness: Human Nature and the Need for Social Connection* (New York: Norton, 2008), 264.

240 "as an explanation for success and for failure": John Swansburg, "The Self-Made Man."

242 "Given that financial rewards can undermine": Tim Kasser and Kennon M. Sheldon, "Time Affluence as a Path Toward Personal Happiness and Ethical Business Practice: Empirical Evidence from Four Studies," *Journal of Business Ethics,* March 18, 2008.

INDEX

INDEX

INDEX

INDEX

ABOUT THE AUTHOR

Celeste Headlee is an award-winning journalist and professional speaker, and is the bestselling author of *We Need to Talk: How to Have Conversations That Matter* and *Heard Mentality*. In her twenty-year career in public radio, she has been the executive producer of *On Second Thought* at Georgia Public Radio and has anchored Natioinal Public Radio's *Tell Me More, Talk of the Nation, All Things Considered, 1A,* and *Weekend Edition.* She also cohosted the national morning news show *The Takeaway* for PRI and WNYC, and anchored World Channel's presidential coverage in 2012. Celeste's TEDx Talk sharing ten ways to have better conversations has had more than 20 million total views to date.

Celeste serves as an advisory board member for procon .org and the Listen First Project and received the 2019 Media Changemaker Award. Along with artist Masud Olufani, Celeste is host of PBS's *Retro Report,* a new weekly series that debuted in fall 2019. She is also cohost of *Men,* season three of the *Scene on Radio* podcast. Her work and insights have been featured on the *Today* show and in various news outlets, including *Psychology Today, Time, Essence, Elle,* BuzzFeed, *Salon,* and

Parade. Celeste has presented to more than one hundred companies, conferences, and universities, including Apple, Google, United Airlines, Duke University, Chobani, and ESPN.

As an NPR host and journalist, Celeste has interviewed hundreds of people from all walks of life. Through her work, she has learned the true power of conversation and its ability to either bridge gaps or deepen wounds. In a time when conversations are often minimized to a few words in a text message and lack of meaningful communication and dialogue abounds, Celeste sheds a much-needed light on the lost and essential art of conversation. As a mixed-race journalist of black and Jewish descent, Celeste also speaks candidly about how to converse on race and other difficult subjects. She lives in Washington, DC.